Endorsements

In a culture overrun by personal slights, reckless blame shifting, and partisan divides, we may find ourselves growing increasingly hostile toward one another, leading to destructive depths of isolation and loneliness. But the way of Jesus offers us a path forward, down the long and winding road of forgiveness. In *Three Strikes, You're Forgiven*, Micah offers us a profound and pastoral road map toward the liberation and freedom we all long for, helping us to, in his words, "discover the scandal of grace to its fullest." This is truly a book for our time.

    JAY Y. KIM
    Pastor and author

Micah offers such an accessible guide to forgiveness, bringing us on a personal journey as well as handing us practical and transformative practices to live freely. Forgiveness can feel so complex, but Micah brings a refreshing simplicity to it. His insightful approach is about finding real freedom that comes with real forgiveness.

    AMY SEIFFERT
    Author of *Grace Looks Amazing on You*, *Starved*, and *Your Name Is Daughter*

In our devastatingly grace-less cancel culture obsessed with the failure of others, Micah helps us see an overwhelmingly grace-full God who transcends time and culture. He shares personal stories of redemption and new opportunities to see others the way God does—with hope and a chance for permanent forgiveness. I am so proud of Micah's willingness to live authentically maskless in a world that encourages facades.

    JENNI WONG CLAYVILLE
    Speaker, teacher, pastor

Despite an abundance of teaching on God's forgiveness in the church, forgiving one another and ourselves is often misunderstood and even more poorly practiced. That's why *Three Strikes, You're Forgiven* is a must-read for all followers of Jesus. With both personal vulnerability and pastoral gentleness, Micah charts a well-informed path to follow on our journey to forgive ourselves and those who've harmed us, and ultimately find peace with God. Our life with God has its most poignant moments when we experience his redemption of our wounds. To this end, Micah has given us a gift in showing how God can repurpose our pain, if we let him.

IKE MILLER, PHD
Author of *Good Baggage* and pastor of Bright City Church

Bitterness and unforgiveness are the two areas I see people get stuck the most in their life and walk with Jesus. It can ooze out like a toxic sludge that taints everything we touch. That's why Micah's new book is a must-read for everyone. His fresh take on the power of forgiveness will unlock paradigm-shifting and life-transforming freedom for your soul.

DAVEY BLACKBURN
Author of *Nothing Is Wasted*, host of the *Nothing Is Wasted* podcast, founder of Nothing is Wasted Ministries

Micah transforms life's most painful moments into a testimony of God's redeeming grace. His words carry both the weight of truth and the balm of hope, offering us a path to healing through the power of forgiveness. This is a book that will leave a lasting imprint on your soul.

DOMINIC DONE
Author of *When Faith Fails* and *Your Longing Has a Name*, founder of PursuingFaith.org

It's hard to imagine a more important task for disciples of Jesus in this cultural moment than learning how to forgive those who've deeply wounded us. While many people ache to experience the freedom of forgiveness, few of us have trusted guides who can share the practices and process that lead us down that path. In reading *Three Strikes, You're Forgiven*, I felt profoundly grateful to companion my friend and fellow pastor Micah as he courageously opened up about his own healing journey of learning that forgiveness, not failure, has the final word for those who follow the way of Jesus. I pray this book blesses you and fills you with the same hope for abundance as it did for me!

BRANDON SHIELDS
Founding pastor of Soma Church, Indianapolis

THREE STRIKES, YOU'RE FORGIVEN

A Tyndale nonfiction imprint

MICAH E.
DAVIS

THREE
STRIKES,
YOU'RE
FORGIVEN

*Encounter a God Who Wants to
Redeem Your Past, Restore Your
Present, and Transform Your Future*

Visit Tyndale online at tyndale.com.

Visit Tyndale Momentum online at tyndalemomentum.com.

Visit the author at micahedavis.com.

Tyndale, Tyndale's quill logo, *Tyndale Momentum*, and the Tyndale Momentum logo are registered trademarks of Tyndale House Ministries. Tyndale Momentum is a nonfiction imprint of Tyndale House Publishers, Carol Stream, Illinois.

Three Strikes, You're Forgiven: Encounter a God Who Wants to Redeem Your Past, Restore Your Present, and Transform Your Future

Copyright © 2025 by Micah Davis. All rights reserved.

Author photo by Garrett and Mikaela Hoppes, copyright © 2024. All rights reserved.

Cover designed by Faceout Studio

Interior designed by Laura Cruise

Edited by Claire Lloyd

Published in association with the literary agency of The Steve Laube Agency.

All Scripture quotations, unless otherwise indicated, are taken from the Holy Bible, *New International Version*,® *NIV*.® Copyright © 1973, 1978, 1984, 2011 by Biblica, Inc.® Used by permission. All rights reserved worldwide.

Scripture quotations marked ESV are from The ESV® Bible (The Holy Bible, English Standard Version®), copyright © 2001 by Crossway, a publishing ministry of Good News Publishers. Used by permission. All rights reserved.

Scripture quotations marked MSG are taken from *The Message*, copyright © 1993, 2002, 2018 by Eugene H. Peterson. Used by permission of NavPress. All rights reserved. Represented by Tyndale House Publishers.

Scripture quotations marked The Voice are taken from The Voice,™ copyright © 2012 by Ecclesia Bible Society. Used by permission. All rights reserved.

The URLs in this book were verified prior to publication. The publisher is not responsible for content in the links, links that have expired, or websites that have changed ownership after that time.

For information about special discounts for bulk purchases, please contact Tyndale House Publishers at csresponse@tyndale.com, or call 1-855-277-9400.

Library of Congress Cataloging-in-Publication Data

A catalog record for this book is available from the Library of Congress.

ISBN 979-8-4005-0140-1

Printed in the United States of America

31	30	29	28	27	26	25
7	6	5	4	3	2	1

To E, who I've watched live the way of forgiveness painfully and repeatedly over the course of life. I know you're still in process, but I'm proud of you.

To T, for showing me that forgiveness really is possible no matter the circumstance. And for proving that the way of reconciliation is a much better way to live than resentment.

To the wounded, the Wounded Healer sees you and loves you. I've written this with you in mind. A forgiving future is coming. Rejoice!

Contents

Author's Note *x*
Foreword *xi*
Prologue: I've Been Through It *1*

PART I: Forgiving Others *9*
    1: The Starting Point *11*
    2: Family Trees *27*
    3: The Cycle of Forgiveness *41*

PART II: Asking for Forgiveness *55*
    4: Transformed Assumptions *57*
    5: Failure Obsessed *73*
    6: Come out of Hiding *87*
    7: Put It to Use *101*

PART III: Forgiving Yourself *117*
    8: Embracing What We Avoid *119*
    9: The Hardest Person to Forgive *131*

PART IV: Forgiving God *147*
    10: The Big Question *149*
    11: A Forgiving Future in a Failing Present *163*
    12: Forgiveness Is for Everyone (Yes, Everyone) *179*
    13: Three Strikes, You're Forgiven *195*

Epilogue: A Legacy That Will Last *207*

Thanks *211*
Appendix A A Note of Consideration Regarding Abuse *215*
Appendix B Verses on Forgiveness *217*
Appendix C Other Helpful Resources *219*
Notes *221*
About *237*

Author's Note

Some of the anecdotal illustrations in this book are true to life and are included with the permission of the persons involved. Names and some details have been changed to protect privacy. All other illustrations are composites of real situations, and any resemblance to people living or dead is purely coincidental.

Foreword

FROM DAY ONE, MICAH STRUCK ME as someone who was not only willing to bear his own wounds but was genuinely committed to helping others find healing too. He has faced moments of devastating loss and, somehow, continues to choose forgiveness, kindness, and a relentless pursuit of God's purpose for his life. His story doesn't minimize the hurt—he's been through it all. Yet, if anything, it has only deepened his love for the God who redeems, restores, and never wastes our pain.

Micah's journey, as you'll read in these pages, is an invitation to reimagine what forgiveness looks like, not just as a spiritual ideal but as a radical act of freedom in the middle of a messy, painful world. This book isn't just about the theory of forgiveness—it's a testament to the gritty, grace-fueled reality of it. In *Three Strikes, You're Forgiven*, Micah invites us to see that forgiveness isn't just a once-and-done process; it's an ongoing cycle of receiving God's grace and learning to extend it, even when we feel like we've got nothing left to give. And his vulnerability in sharing his story is itself an act of courage.

As a pastor, I've had the privilege of walking with people who are wrestling with similar questions: How do we forgive the unforgivable? How do we find peace when life feels like a series of unhealed wounds? And, even more pointedly, how do we find forgiveness for ourselves? Micah comes to these questions not from a place of detached expertise but from his own life experience. He doesn't claim to have all the answers, but in these pages he offers the kind of wisdom that only comes from personal relationship with a God who turns even our greatest failures into moments of redemptive beauty.

The message of forgiveness is one that resonates deeply with all of us who have found ourselves wondering if God's mercy really can stretch far enough to cover our worst moments. Maybe you're carrying a deep hurt from someone close to you, or perhaps you're weighed down by your own mistakes. Either way, this book is a reminder that there is a God who sees you, who knows the weight of your pain, and who calls you not just to survive it but to find freedom on the other side of it.

I've often said in my own ministry, "The most painful parts of your story may be the most life-giving part of someone else's." Micah understands this truth deeply because he's lived it. In these pages, he doesn't shy away from sharing the hard parts—his struggles with identity, the sting of betrayal, the years spent unraveling lies he believed about himself. And in doing so, he creates space for readers to be honest about their own stories too.

Micah's journey reminds me of the times in my own life when I've wrestled with the tension between cynicism and hope. Cynicism, as I've written before, is often rooted in a self-protective scarcity mindset. But hope—true hope—requires trust. And trust is where forgiveness begins. Forgiveness asks us to release control, to trust that God is working even when we can't see it, and to believe that redemption is possible even in the most broken circumstances.

Micah writes with this kind of hope. His words remind us that the gospel isn't just good news for our eternity—it's good news for our past and present too. It tells us that failure doesn't have to be final, that our wounds don't have to define us, and that no one is beyond the reach of God's grace. This story is a testament to that truth.

One of the things I admire most about Micah's writing is his ability to bring theology to life. In this book, he writes about the four dimensions of forgiveness: forgiving others, being forgiven by others, forgiving yourself, and forgiving God. Each one is explored not just as a concept but as a lived reality. Micah doesn't pretend that forgiveness is easy. He acknowledges the deep scars that life can leave and the courage it takes to let go of resentment. But he also reminds us that forgiveness isn't something we have to muster up on our own. It's a gift we receive from God, one that empowers us to offer grace even when it feels impossible.

This book isn't one of sanitized faith or easy answers. It's messy, raw, and relatable. And that's what makes it so powerful. In these pages, you'll walk through the complexities of forgiving others, the difficulty of forgiving yourself, and perhaps the most daunting challenge of all—trusting a God who sometimes feels distant. But make no mistake: this isn't a story of despair. It's a story of redemption and hope, written by someone who has chosen to live a life shaped by both.

As Micah shares stories that are achingly real and beautifully raw, he doesn't shy away from the hard questions or the complex emotions that come with forgiveness, nor does he gloss over the painful process of healing. He's honest about the mess, the setbacks, and the days when moving forward feels impossible. But he's also unwavering in his conviction that God's love has the power to transform even the most broken parts of our lives.

Transparency is a rare gift in a world that often treats faith as a performance. Micah's message of forgiveness reminds us that true freedom in Christ isn't about looking the part or saying the right things; it's about bringing our whole, unvarnished selves to a God who already knows us completely. In a culture that's quick to condemn and slow to forgive, this message is a deeply needed breath of fresh air. We are called to a countercultural way of living that chooses compassion over judgment, humility over pride, and forgiveness over bitterness.

Micah and I have had countless conversations about the beauty and the difficulty of following Jesus. We've wrestled with what it means to love well, to forgive freely, and to trust deeply even when life doesn't make sense. And through all of it, I've been inspired by his unwavering faith, his relentless hope, and his commitment to seeing others set free. This book is a powerful reminder that God's grace is always greater than our failures, that forgiveness is possible even in the darkest of circumstances, and that redemption is real—even when we can't see it yet.

So, if you're holding this book, wondering if there's really hope for you, know this: you're not alone. Micah's story is here to remind you that you are seen, loved, and forgiven by a God who delights in making all things new. This journey won't be easy, but I promise you it's worth it. And as you read Micah's story, may you find the courage to let God into your own story too, to let him work in the hidden, hurting places of your heart, and to trust that forgiveness—even when it feels like the hardest thing in the world—can truly set you free.

As you read this book, I hope you'll see yourself in its pages. Maybe you'll recognize the places where you've been hurt or the moments when you've struggled to let go of resentment. Maybe you'll see your own reflection in the parts that wrestle with shame and self-doubt. But more than anything, I hope you'll encounter the God who meets us in our mess, who transforms our pain into purpose, and who whispers to each of us, "Three strikes—you're forgiven." My prayer is that the words in this book will set hearts free, bring healing to broken places, and draw people closer to the God who makes all things new. My prayer is that these pages will help countless others discover the beauty of a life lived in the light of God's forgiveness.

Ian Simkins
Lead pastor at The Bridge Church

Prologue

I've Been Through It

THERE WAS A TIME WHEN I thought my world was falling apart. There was a time when I thought God was distant and didn't care. There was a time when I thought the future—and my life on earth that encompassed it—was pointless. Actually . . . there have been many times when a version of those narratives has run through my head.

Can you relate?

———

October 16, 2005, was the worst day of my ten-year-old life.

We had just returned home from Sunday morning service. Dad had given the sermon, and people had been saved. All seemed right in the world. Until it wasn't.

A few minutes later, a scream so loud that it echoed through our house sent me sprinting down the staircase. Turns out it was Mom. Thankfully, she was okay (physically), but her heart had been ripped out.

The next thing I knew, my dad was walking out the front door with a pile of clothes under one arm and some dry cleaning draped over the other.

Later that night, there was a crowd of people in our living room. Elders, board members, extended family, and other confidants consoled my mom. As I sat in the other room, I could faintly pick up what was being discussed.

". . . moral failure."

"He's done . . ."

"Yes, with her . . ."

"I don't know where he is. He says he's quitting the church, our family, and God."

"This is really bad . . ."

Dad was leaving to live another life with his mistress. He was leaving behind the life he no longer wanted. He was leaving *me*.[1]

Déjà Vu

Ten years later, I sat in a packed van with a moving truck in tow winding around the city that my family had called home for the past six years—Nashville, Tennessee. This was a place of restoration and renewal for us.

A few months after that fateful October day, after endless hours of intense, excruciating marital and family counseling, my parents renewed their marriage vows and committed to a new way of life, together. However, my dad's decision carried consequences. For four years my dad moved into the secular workforce in an attempt to rebuild the trust and respect that he had desecrated.

Eventually, my godfather called my dad and invited him to move from Indiana and reenter vocational ministry by joining the staff of his church in Nashville. At the time, it was one of the fastest growing churches in the country according to *Outreach Magazine*.

For those next few years, life was a dream. My formative years were spent within a thick web of community. Routine trips to my godfather's house and farm ingrained sweet memories into my mind. He was someone I looked up to, emulated, and wanted to follow. There was no one who shaped my view of and love for God more. To this day, I still have nearly one hundred of his sermon outlines in a memory box.

Our church sits downtown, catty-corner to the Tennessee Titans stadium. The drive on the interstate provides a view that intersects our church's sign and the Nissan Stadium sign.

I always loved that view. However, on this particular day, I knew that view would come to signify something different to me moving forward. No longer was this church the spiritual haven that I'd called home. No longer was my dad pastoring there. No longer was it the community I felt I belonged to.

Instead, we were off to Indianapolis, Indiana. I was headed back to my home state for college to play basketball and start my journey toward adulthood and independence. The rest of my family was off to pursue a dream that had been stirring in their hearts for years to plant a church on the city's north side.

In the rearview was the church that I had come to know and love over the last six years, but it was also a church that would never be the same.

A few months earlier, my parents had become aware of some questionable moral decisions my godfather—my dad's best friend who was also our pastor—was making. My parents decided to confront him.

That night, my dad pleaded with his friend to reconsider his choices. But his mind was made up. He was following in my dad's footsteps.

He was leaving his church and family to live with his mistress. He was leaving behind the life he no longer wanted. He was leaving *me*.

Why Micah E. Davis?

If I had a dollar for every time someone asked me about my middle initial . . . well, I wouldn't need to keep writing books to earn a living.

My middle name is Edward. I was named after my paternal grandfather who was affectionately known as "Ed" and my maternal grandfather whose middle name is . . . you guessed it . . . Edward. For years I idolized both of these men as the patriarchs of our beautifully broken family.

However, when I was thirteen, my family found out that my dad's dad was not his biological dad. In fact, he had adopted my dad as a young child—a secret that was concealed for more than three decades. Not only was he not my biological grandfather, but he was living an entirely separate life full of scandalous escapades and excursions. He and my grandmother divorced after more than three decades of marriage.

Twelve years later, I sat on my parents' back porch, reliving the entire script as my mom shared that her dad was not her biological dad. Only *this* time around? My grandfather didn't know either. It was a secret that had been concealed from him and my mom for almost five decades.

So much hurt and pain ensued as I watched my parents pick up the shattered pieces of the identity they once knew.

When I was offered the opportunity to write my first book, I knew that I wanted my pen name to include my middle initial.[2] Edward was a middle name that for years I thought about changing.

I want nothing to do with this lineage.

I want nothing to do with this name.

I want nothing to do with these men.

They've abandoned me.

But I had an epiphany one day. *What if what Satan meant for evil, God could use for good?*[3] So, the middle initial stuck as a reminder that when other people fail, God never does.

What's the Point?

In the last two decades of my life, I've watched father figure after father figure fail. In fact, as I'm writing this sentence, another article has dropped revealing that the pastor of the church that founded my high school (a formative leader in my own life and walk with Jesus over the years) has just had his resignation accepted by his congregation for what's been deemed to be a bullying and intimidating leadership style.

Sigh.

I've experienced some of the worst pain imaginable. I've felt hurt, betrayed, and abandoned. I've been lied to. I've been dismissed. I've been wounded beyond measure.

And yet . . .

I have witnessed God—the Great Healer—show up time after time.

In the moments when I've desperately wanted to choose cynicism, I've instead fought hard to cultivate compassion. In the moments when I've longed for revenge, I've prayed for justice and mercy to win out. In the moments when I've felt betrayed, I've found refuge in a God who sees me.[4] In the moments when I've witnessed a world equate failure with finality, I've experienced—firsthand—a God who redeems our failure for his glory.

We cannot follow Jesus and *not* press further into the concept of forgiveness. Here's Jesus of Nazareth in Matthew 6: "For if you forgive other people when they sin against you, your heavenly Father will also forgive you. But if you do not forgive others their sins, your Father will not forgive your sins."[5]

That's a pretty explicit causal statement.

If, then.

If, then.

I have failed over and over again. I've had others fail me over and over again. And yet . . . I've discovered a God who's with me in the furnace. I've discovered a God who's faithful when others aren't. I've discovered a God who reigns over it all. And—with all that I have—I hope to help you discover that God too.

Within Jesus' two-sentence imperative on forgiveness are four necessary acts:

1. Our need to forgive others
2. Our need to be forgiven by others
3. Our need to forgive ourselves
4. Our need to forgive a forgiving God

That is the journey we are invited to go on. On the other side of forgiveness is freedom—the freedom that you've been desperately longing for. It's possible to receive, but it comes at a cost. And it's a price worth paying every single time.

When I was in third grade, I played baseball for the first and last time. It was the first year of what's referred to as "live pitching," where the players themselves pitch. I played for the Noblesville Yankees. I was stoked to get to don such a legendary logo. Every time I laced up my cleats, I'd imagine I was Derek Jeter on deck at Yankee Stadium.

Unfortunately, the season was a disaster. I was the only kid on the team who never got a chance to "live pitch." My coach kindly but clearly communicated that my arm wasn't strong enough. I was a year younger than all of my peers and developmentally wasn't close to being able to hang with the older kids. I was relegated to right field (the area of a baseball field where one is least likely to be involved in the action). I also spent the entire season swinging and missing.

That's right. The entire season, I never got a hit. Well, that's not technically true. The last game of the season, I contributed to a run via a "sacrifice bunt" where I (honestly accidentally) allowed my bat to make brief contact with the ball, allowing a teammate to score. Later in that game, I also was "walked" and eventually found myself "stealing" home on an errant throw. It was exhilarating.

But the rest of the season? Bat after bat . . . it was the same story over and over again.

I would swing and miss. Swing and miss. Swing and miss.

And every time, the teenage, minimum-wage umpire would cruelly caw, "Three strikes, you'reeeeee out!"

Perhaps you're picking up this book, holding your breath at the idea that you—*you* of *all* people—could ever be forgiven for what you've done. Maybe you're filled with shame, regret, or embarrassment for the failures of your past. Maybe you feel like your life has consisted of strikeout after strikeout.

Friend, whatever it is that you've done, whatever it is that you fell short in, whatever it is that you messed up, God *forgives* you. As high as the heavens are above the earth, as far as the east is from the west, so great is his mercy . . . to you and to me. You are forgiven—in Christ Jesus—saved by the blood of the Cross.

The pages ahead—I believe—will be a respite for your soul. No matter what you've done or what's been done to you, there exists a *better* way. It is not a way devoid of suffering or pain. It is not an easy three-step process. It is a journey full of starts and stops. Two steps forward and three steps back. It is a *long*, narrow way. But it is a way of breakthrough, of healing, and of triumph.

It's the way of Jesus. To you and to me, he offers an invitation.

> Are you tired? Worn out? Burned out on religion? Come to me. Get away with me and you'll recover your life. I'll show you how to take a real rest. Walk with me and work

with me—watch how I do it. Learn the unforced rhythms of grace. I won't lay anything heavy or ill-fitting on you. Keep company with me and you'll learn to live freely and lightly.[6]

When the going gets tough . . .

When the odds are stacked against you . . .

When you've been let down repeatedly . . .

When you've failed over and over again . . . the Umpire of life's voice screams out, "Three strikes, you'reeeeee . . . *forgiven*."

Let us journey together to uncover the balm those healing words can become.

PART I

FORGIVING

OTHERS

1
THE STARTING POINT

MY SENIOR YEAR OF HIGH SCHOOL was the only time that I was able to call myself a "multi-sport athlete." For the first eighteen years of my life, I was strictly what we'd call a "hooper" (that's a basketball player for all you uncultured folk). However, my calculus teacher was also the track coach, and—after I had signed my letter of intent to play basketball in college—I suddenly had a spring sports season with nothing to immediately prepare for. My calculus teacher—soon-to-be coach—seized the opportunity and said, "Why don't you come try out for the track team?"

So, one Thursday afternoon, I found myself in a pair of borrowed cleats, feeling claustrophobic and uncomfortably exposed in nothing but a tracksuit (the spandex kind, not the warm-up kind). I was told to line up on a pair of blocks, which supposedly would help me get off to a faster start in the race. As I looked to my left and right, no one was next to me. In fact, the person to my right was ahead of me and the person to my left was behind me.

"Hey, Coach, what's up with this? Why do they get to start ahead of me? Are they cheating?"

My coach—attempting not to laugh me off the track—patiently explained.

"No, everyone begins at a different starting point, but the track condenses and eventually evens out to where everyone runs the full four hundred meters."

I didn't understand but nodded as if I did. The gun went off, and the race started.

Being in the outside lane, I took off. I felt so far ahead of everyone else. But then, a funny thing happened: those on the inside lanes began to catch up, and eventually they started to pass me. Finally, on the back straightaway, we all ended up in a similar position as we jockeyed for a photo finish.

Over time and many races later, I came to understand. Track rules are clear that each four-hundred-meter runner starts in a different position and must stay in their lane for the entire lap. This is intentional because it allows those in the outside lane to run the same distance. The different starting points actually diminish the competitive advantage for those in the inside lanes.

When it comes to a topic like forgiveness, we're all starting in different positions. Some of us are in an inside lane, having experienced minimal amounts of relational strife and hurt up to this point in our lives. Others of us are further ahead. We've lived more life, experienced more hurt, and have wider curves to navigate. Perhaps you find yourself somewhere in between.

Regardless of our starting point, we're all running the same race. And that race is toward a finish line of forgiveness. At different points in the race (seasons of life) forgiveness may feel like a breeze. It's a practice that may come naturally or easily. Other times, forgiveness may feel like a ten-ton weight dragging us down and holding us back. We may see those in other lanes passing us. But eventually, the path to the finish line will even out. On the other side of the finish line will be a garden city where everyone who has ever run well[1] will be welcomed into an everlasting reality of goodness, truth, and beauty.

There's a reason we have to stay in our own lane in a track race. It's so we don't trip up or accidentally hurt anyone else. The Way, the Truth, and the Life that is Jesus Christ is the boundary of our lane. It is through his teachings that we're able to understand and come to terms with our starting point, run our race freely and cleanly, and finish with a forgiving—not a bitter, cynical, or resentful—heart.

"Wait, wait, wait. Micah, are you telling me that I'm supposed to just pretend like nothing happened? That what he did to me didn't occur? And I'm supposed to move on?"

I was a nervous barely-there-twenty-three-year-old youth pastor in the suburbs of Indianapolis sitting across the table from a high school freshman boy. For weeks, we had been meeting to talk through his painful past. How he was abused and abandoned by his birth parents, adopted by his new parents, and caught in this tragic in-between of an old life he hated but desperately wanted and a new life he loved but desperately wanted to leave. Some of the same struggles his biological parents had wrestled with were beginning to surface in this young man's life.

I was roughly four months into my first ministry position, and I had virtually no formal counseling training. Whatever I had said clearly did not translate well, so I walked it back.

"No. No. No. Please don't misunderstand me. I'm not in any way attempting to diminish the trauma or pain you've gone through. I'm trying to help you see how that pain and trauma is now informing the present actions you're taking. And I want to see you step into the future God has for you by allowing him to redeem your past in this present moment. The past cannot be revised, but it can be redeemed."

I sat back, sipping on my one-dollar McDonald's sweet tea and letting him stew on my one-liner that would make Craig Groeschel offer me a fist bump.

"Well, how do I do that?"

I wasn't ready for that question . . .

The truth is many of us are coming to these pages with vastly different scripts of life. Forgiveness and reconciliation are not as cut-and-dried as "because the Bible tells me so." There is a mountain of complexity that must be sorted through, tended to, and cared for in this process.[2]

I want to give space and dignity to those of you who have endured really difficult events throughout your life. I believe in a God who sees. I believe in a God who cares. And I believe in a God who wants to partner with you in putting back together the broken pieces of your life. But I also understand that platitudes and clichés will not soothe the pain many of us are wrestling with.

Forgiveness is not a formula. It is a crucible.

It is a crucible that burns and refines all the muck and mess we have incurred over the course of this life. And it can be painful. Pulling off the bandages we often cover our wounds with is so difficult. But sometimes the scabs need to be exposed so that healing can take place.

The whole of our lives comes down to what we do with our pain. An invitation exists to allow our pain to be transformed rather than transferred. Forgiveness—and to a greater degree, reconciliation—is only possible if we first allow past pain to be healed rather than to cause harm.

We've already established that we live in a broken world. Our brokenness as a society manifests in four key areas: sin, damage, weakness, and wounds.[3]

Sin

Sin, at its core, is a failure to love and trust God, which leads to a failure to love and trust our neighbor. Sin often comes from the disordered desires of our heart, twisting our allegiance to things that are outright evil or, more subtly, turning seemingly good things into "god" things. To sin literally means to miss the mark. Paul tells us in Romans that "all have sinned and fall short of the glory of God" and "the wages of sin is death."[4] It is sin that separates us from God. And sin manifests in a multitude of ways that run contrary to the fruits of the Spirit.[5]

Damage

There are systems—both internal and external—which are frayed, fractured, and underdeveloped. We see this manifest in the outworking of systematic injustice: poverty, racism, sexism, and more. These damaged systems created the "haves" and "have nots" among us. As a result of the world's damaged systems, there is a disparity and inequality among whole people groups.

Weakness

On an individual level, in our fallibility, we all carry inherent weaknesses. There are aspects of our stories, family histories, wirings, and personalities that contribute to the makeup of these weaknesses. Each of us is prone to particular sin patterns and damaged structures that stem from the weaknesses of what the Scriptures call our *sarx* (flesh).

Wounds

The final layer of societal brokenness is our wounds. Wounds develop from the hurt or harm caused by our own sinful actions or the actions of others. Wounds encompass much of the pain we've incurred over time and can manifest in small or large ways. They can be severe or surface level or anywhere in between.

The most physically damaging time of my life occurred during my sophomore year of college. We were roughly three games into the basketball season, and I was on the brink of some increased playing time. I had worked extremely hard over the course of the summer to improve my skills and ready myself for more responsibility on the team.

One day in practice, I was playing defense against my teammate Joel (pronounced Jo-L). Joel was in incredible physical shape. He was bigger, faster, stronger, and better-looking[6] than me. I had to do whatever I could to compensate for my limitations against him. To do that, as Joel's teammate came over to screen me in order to free him up for a shot, I slid under the screen, foreseeing it, in an effort to cut him off. The problem was, I was low in a defensive stance. (Coach T would have been proud of that. This was a rarity in my collegiate career.) Joel was also low in a driving stance. On the other side of the screen, we collided.

His tooth sunk into the skin right above my eye.

Blood was everywhere. Joel's tooth was on the ground. And we were both rushed to the training room where I got stitches and Joel sat toothless.[7]

Now, I know what you're thinking: *that's not that bad*. You're right.

So fast-forward two days to when we have a recruit on campus. As an underclassman, I'm summoned to the gym for a workout with this recruit. We finish the workout playing one-on-one, and on game point, he drives his shoulder straight into my lower lip, which causes my tooth to drive through it.

Once again, blood was everywhere. The tooth was safe. But my lip would swell up to look like I had been stung by a bee . . . or ten.

A week later, beginning to look like Scott Sterling, I was in practice driving the ball, and as I got into the lane, a teammate on defense swiped down. Instead of making contact with the ball, he hit my pinkie finger, which was crushed under the weight of the impact.

I will never forget looking down and seeing my injured pinkie finger. My face went pale and my body went numb as I tried to process what I was looking at. It was physically traumatic.[8]

Once again, I was immediately rushed to the training room where our head trainer had to set my finger back in place. It was extremely painful. I ended up in the emergency room where a full dislocation was assessed, and I was instructed to keep a splint on for four weeks.

Two weeks later, I was playing in our final game before Thanksgiving break. I had missed the last few games with all of these injuries, and it felt more painful to sit out and watch. So I dismissed the doctor's orders, heavy-taped my left hand, and began to practice.

That game saw our team with a large lead in the second half. My coach told me to check in. I did, and two possessions later, I was once again chasing someone off of a screen. Only this time, instead of a five-foot-ten-inch physical specimen in Joel, I was chasing a six-foot-seven-inch string bean named Charlie. Charlie was one of the other team's better shooters, and I knew that I needed to stick close by. I "chased" him, sticking right behind him. In an effort to free himself from my impeccable[9] defense, he chicken winged me with that long, lanky arm. The problem? His elbow made contact with my mouth. That's right.

Once again, blood was everywhere. This time, *my* tooth was on the ground.

In a two-week time frame I busted my eye, cut open my lip, broke my finger, and lost my big front tooth. I still find myself having physical reactions when holding a basketball in a particular way. In fact, I was never the same on the basketball court after that two-week stretch. I was terrified of contact, and I hated stepping closer to the basket than the three-point line.

Perhaps you've been fed the lie that life with Jesus was supposed to make everything good, easy, and right. An oft-misused line from Jesus is given as evidence: "For my yoke is easy and my burden is light."[10]

But the word "easy" there, in Greek, is *chrēstos*, and it literally means "useful, good, pleasant, better."[11]

My friends, the way of Jesus is *not* an easy way. In fact, most statements on following Jesus in the Scriptures center around just how *difficult* it is. Why wouldn't it be? It's counterculture to the world we live in. Constantly, Jesus exemplifies a *better* way. A way of life and life to the full.

Here's another line from Jesus in John 16: "I have told you these things, so that in me you may have peace. In this world you will have trouble. But take heart! I have overcome the world."[12]

That word, "trouble," is, in Greek, *thlipsis*. It means "suffering."[13] And its range of uses are on a spectrum from everyday wounding to intense persecution. In other words, the hard knocks of life.[14] This term denotes distress and anguish. And Jesus says we will face such hardship.

But . . . take heart.

Grammatically, Jesus offers this phrase to his disciples as an imperative or a command. In other words, when the hard knocks of life come our way, we are offered a better way. The power of the Holy Spirit gives us the ability to take heart.

Please hear me. This is not to trivialize or excuse away your pain and suffering. It is to offer you hope that there can be life on the other side of it.

We must handle each individual story with great care. But no story is too far from redemption. This is the Good News of the gospel of Jesus Christ. In Jesus, we are offered an alternative to the story of our trauma and pain.

There is a way forward. In a world that thirsts for retribution, followers of Jesus can pursue reconciliation. In a world of intense division, followers of Jesus can seek holistic integration of mind, soul, and body. In a world that thrives on hate, followers of Jesus can find healing in a God who saves. Healing of our pain is possible. There's nothing that heals us like the blood of Jesus.

The prophet Isaiah notes, "Surely he took up our pain and bore our suffering, yet we considered him punished by God, stricken by him, and afflicted. But he was pierced for our transgressions, he was crushed for our iniquities; the punishment that brought us peace was on him, and by his wounds we are healed."[15]

This is not an ethereal divine being disconnected from the reality of our broken world. This is a God who got down in the dirt and experienced—to the greatest degree—all the hurt, pain, and suffering you and I have ever endured.

Think about this: On the cross, Jesus took on the weight of all sin for all time. The worst of the worst things that have happened to you, Jesus died for. Jesus bore that to the nth degree. We cannot even fathom the pain he endured. But he certainly didn't hold back from expressing it: "At three in the afternoon Jesus cried out in a loud voice, *'Eloi, Eloi, lema sabachthani?'* (which means 'My God, my God, why have you forsaken me?')."[16]

In Jesus, we find our wounds and suffering exposed, enveloped, and transformed by the wounded sufferer himself. As a mentor of mine once said, "Jesus' method [of healing] isn't protection against pain but redemption through pain."[17]

All of this can sound neat and cozy if we keep it on the margins of our life. But true transformation only comes through doing the work. We are not responsible for awful, traumatic things that have been done to us. But we are responsible for tenderly caring for our wounds and allowing our pain to be touched by Jesus—who himself understands pain and wounds unlike any other.

This brings us back to the question I was asked at McDonald's all those years ago. "Well, how do I do that?"

In my experience, I've never been able to work through painful, traumatic events on my own. Breakthrough has often come after I have vulnerably opened myself up to other brothers and sisters who could receive me as I was and reflect back to me my true self in Christ. Who this has included has shifted from season to season, but community has always been an integral part of the healing process.

I've also needed professional help from experienced, licensed counselors. Over the years, I have benefitted greatly from Christian counselors who took their practice and their faith seriously. These men and women knew God's Word, and their counsel and direction came from the overflow of their union with God. I have leaned on these sages as I've tried to put together the fragmented pieces of my past—including all the painful parts (physically, emotionally, and mentally) of an athletic career that had sapped a great deal of self-confidence and replaced it with bitter cynicism.

All throughout the Scriptures, we see a God who engages every sense and aspect of our humanity to get to us. As God reveals himself, so too are we revealed. And as we reveal ourselves, so too is God revealed. This is the beauty of a counseling space, where our true self can be discovered and carefully tended to by someone with the expertise to help us navigate the unexplored, painful parts of our past in hopes of discovering a healthier way forward.

This can often be an arduous process. Perhaps you've given counseling a try before, and it wasn't a good fit or you had a poor experience. If I could gently encourage you, try again. And again. And again. It is worth the effort.

But if counseling isn't possible for you currently, practices like prayer journaling, confession with a trusted friend, or seeking wisdom from a spiritual mentor like a pastor or small group leader could be a great place to start.

Over the last few years in particular, I have focused on receiving spiritual direction from one of the wisest, most-loving, most-Jesus-like people I know. Her guidance and care for me has been invaluable. But it took time to develop that relationship.

So if you find yourself in a space of disorientation or pain from your past, may I encourage you to seek counsel? Don't process your pain alone. Let God reveal himself to you as you reveal yourself to another *imago* Dei.[18]

In John 20, Jesus has risen from the dead and appears before his disciples. All but one: Thomas, also known as Didymus ("the twin"). When Thomas returns, the disciples enthusiastically share, "We have seen the Lord!"[19]

Thomas, ever the realist, comes back with a snarky reply. "Unless I see the nail marks in his hands and put my finger where the nails were, and put my hand into his side, I will not believe."[20]

Oh, Thomas.

Most of us know Thomas for this line. He's been unaffectionately termed "doubting Thomas." But I don't think Thomas gets nearly enough credit for the *faith* he's shown before this moment.

A little backstory: a few chapters earlier, there's this oft-overlooked exchange between Jesus and his disciples prior to Lazarus's resurrection in John 11. It goes like this: "Then [Jesus] said to his disciples, 'Let us go back to Judea.' 'But Rabbi,' they said, 'a short while ago the Jews there tried to stone you, and yet you are going back?'"[21]

Translation: this is not a good idea, Jesus. We don't want you to do that.

But Jesus was indignant. *Lazarus is dead. I'm going back to comfort his sisters and fulfill my Kingdom agenda. All aboard?*

. . . crickets.

Except Thomas. Doubting Thomas. "Then Thomas (also known as Didymus) said to the rest of the disciples, 'Let us also go, that we may die with him.'"[22]

Thomas was so attuned to Jesus and his agenda that he was willing to die with him. He believed Jesus was the foretold Messiah. So when Jesus was brutally murdered and buried, all of Thomas's dreams were dashed. He had believed so fiercely. He'd been let down so embarrassingly.

Thomas's response to the other disciples was him doing what we're all naturally inclined to do: not make the same mistake twice. Jesus' death was traumatic for his disciples. They had mortgaged everything on him being who he said he was. And he was gone. Just like that.

Devotion had turned into disillusionment. Life as they knew it had been forever upended.

Perhaps you can recall the day your life changed forever. You can remember the sights, sounds, and scene of your biggest failure, your deepest shame, your greatest nightmare. And you find yourself disappointed and disenchanted with a God who said he would save you but has seemingly abandoned you.

I think Thomas understood what that's like. For eight days, he lived in total darkness. A new reality had set in. A reality full of hurt, embarrassment, frustration, and resentment.

This is not the life I signed up for, I imagine Thomas thinking.

And then, "A week later [Jesus'] disciples were in the house again, and Thomas was with them. Though the doors were locked, Jesus came and stood among them and said, 'Peace be with you!' Then he said to Thomas, 'Put your finger here; see my hands. Reach out your hand and put it into my side. Stop doubting and believe.'"[23]

The question we might leave this story with is *Why did Jesus wait?* It's the same question we're all asking in our own stories.

Why hasn't Jesus shown up?

Why hasn't Jesus healed me?

Why hasn't Jesus initiated justice for the wrongs done to me?

The trauma of our past often keeps us in a pit of despair that slowly dismisses the possibility of healing ever taking place. But in time, the Wounded Healer reveals himself, scars intact.

He's waited for this moment. The moment when the pain of the world, the pain he endured, and the pain of your own past all coalesce. A moment of desperation when Jesus most clearly reveals himself to you.

There's a painting by Caravaggio called *The Incredulity of Saint Thomas* that beautifully depicts this scene. Here we have Jesus gently guiding Thomas's finger into his wound. And we have Thomas with an expression of such surprise and intensity that it forces us to fix our gaze on Thomas and ponder the thoughts going through his brain.

This is a moment of epiphany.

Jesus really is who he says he is. That truth has moved from the theoretical to the actual. Jesus encounters Thomas in the most personal and intimate way. He meets Thomas's wounds with his own. And it is this encounter that changes everything for Thomas.

Thomas said to him, "My Lord and my God!"[24]

Thomas's life had been upended by the disappointment of the Savior's death and disappearance. But Thomas's life is even more upended by the encounter not of an empty tomb but of a risen Lord. This is the power that Jesus possesses. He's able to take all the pain, all the hurt, all the trauma—wherever it may be on the sliding scale of life—and not just defeat it, not just resurrect it, but repurpose it. According to Jesus, the wounds of this life do not disappear; they transform.

Trauma is redeemed not through avoidance or expiration but through encounter, through an alternative story that is entrusted to a loving, wise Savior in the context of relationship.

If all we believe about God is that he is a Savior who lived, died, was resurrected, and ascended, that is certainly enough to get us saved. But when we also believe this alternative story is not just universal, but personal, that the invitation is extended to us to touch Jesus' wounds and see for ourselves that he really is who he says he is, that's what gets us healed.

I love the picture titled *Healing of Peter's Mother-in-Law* from the great artist Rembrandt, who depicts Jesus healing her. It's a raw sketch of a tender Savior coming to the aid and picking up a dying woman. She is deathly sick. And yet, Jesus' immediate reaction is to touch her. "He touched her hand and the fever left her."[25]

No thought of whether he would attract the sickness. No thought of if he should or could heal her. No fear or resignation of whether showing up was the right thing to do. Jesus' immediate response was to encounter this woman in her disease.

Sin is a disease that has infected us all. It has manifested in our broken systems, our personal weaknesses, and our wounds. The outworking of sin has—at its worst—exposed a large multitude of us to trauma in this life. Events that make forgiveness and reconciliation feel as improbable as a resurrected encounter.

And yet, the Wounded Healer himself stands among us. "Peace be with you!"[26]

The invitation to touch his wounds is given.

Your trauma is true. Your pain is real. It should be handled with great care.

Also, Jesus really did die on a cross. He really was buried. And he really did rise from the grave. He offers us the chance to not just believe that he is Lord but to encounter him for ourselves. To "taste and see that the LORD is good."[27]

On the other side of an encounter like that, doubt becomes belief, hurt becomes hope, and the trauma of the past is transformed into redemptive scars.

The scars of your past do not disqualify you from experiencing forgiveness and reconciliation. The scars of your past are the evidence that your wounds have been healed by Jesus, singularly empowering you to extend and experience forgiveness and reconciliation in an upside-down, backwards, Kingdom sort of way. Oh, what good news this is.

It is the grace of Jesus Christ covering us that allows us all to run the race. A race that seeks to redeem our past, restore our present, and secure our future.

On your mark . . .

Get set . . .

2

FAMILY TREES

I HAVE ALWAYS BEEN A PEOPLE PLEASER.

As I've done the work attempting to uncover some of my inner wiring and motivations through counseling and therapy, I have come to believe that it was embedded in me as a child. I'm the oldest of five kids. I am extremely type A. And I'm an Enneagram 3 (that's an achiever-type for those of you not well-versed).

In other words, I'm the kind of people pleaser they'd make in a lab.

So, of course, I can recollect the summer prior to my freshman year of high school, when my people-pleasing tendency had reached an inflection point.

I had tried out and somehow made the top AAU basketball team in the state of Tennessee. I still remember tryouts. Two grueling days at Smyrna High School. Twenty-five kids were invited. Eight of us made the team.

You have to believe me when I say that I was more surprised than anybody. I was shorter, smaller, and less athletic than all of my teammates, but I was on the team.

However, my roster spot only increased the internal pressure I felt.

I had everything to prove *and* everything to lose. It was a recipe for disaster.

Supposedly, Disney World is the place to "create magical memories to last a lifetime."[1] However, the summer prior to my freshman year of high school, Disney World became less magical memory and more living nightmare.

For every eighth grader, AAU nationals at Disney World is a rite of passage in the basketball world. This is the equivalent to the Little League World Series. It is *the* tournament that everyone aspires to play in. LeBron James and his eighth-grade teammates even played in this tournament back in the day.[2] There is no greater stage.

My dad and I ended up making the trek down to Orlando from Nashville together and timed it out to visit Universal Studios prior to the tournament starting. This was supposed to be the trip of our lives.[3]

My team's Elite 8 game had us matched up against the number two team in the country. As I reflect on that game, I can count on both hands the number of guys who ended up playing at a high level in college. The talent was out of this world.

Our first half wasn't pretty. We found ourselves down big, and I had yet to check into the game. I was starting to get tense, and thoughts were racing through my head.

Why haven't I checked in yet?

What have I done wrong?

Why is this happening?

To make matters worse, the only other kid who played my position was the coach's son. I was a wreck internally. Remember, we only had eight players on our roster. That was intentional. It *forced* our coaches to play everyone. Everyone except . . . *me*.

The second half started, and we were down one guy to an injury. Seven players left. Our starters were gassed. The other team was fresh and running us right out of the gym.

Eventually, we found ourselves down fifteen, then twenty, then thirty. The clock began dwindling: ten minutes, five minutes, one minute left.

The final buzzer sounded, and I sat frozen in my chair . . . not sure if I was ever going to get up.

At some point, the teams lined up to shake hands at center court. Everyone except me. I walked right past that line. In fact, I walked across the court, past my team, up the bleachers, and began sprinting out of the Disney's Wide World of Sports Complex altogether.

When I got outside, I ripped my jersey off and began dry heaving on the concrete. Eventually, I heard a voice. "Micah! Micah! Stop."

It was my dad. He was crying too.

As soon as I saw him, I collapsed into his arms and began weeping.

I'll never forget what he said to me in that moment. His six-foot-four-inch frame bent down to whisper into my ear. "Micah, this is going to be a decisive moment in your life. You can either walk away now and live with bitterness in your heart the rest of your life, or you can walk back in with your head held high, *forgive* them, and use this experience to fuel you."

I did go back in. And I did try to hold my head up high and receive consolation from other parents and teammates. I wish I could say that I immediately forgave my coach, but I didn't. It was a wound that stuck with me for the rest of my basketball career.

A wound that made any slight or shrewd remark by a coach set me off and think that they were out to get me.

A wound that I carried for so many years without any path forward.

A wound that I failed to forget.

How do you forgive someone when you can't seem to forget the hurt they've caused? I wrestled with this tension internally for years.

Eventually, my wound began to spread and project onto other people. No coach believed in me. No coach thought I was good enough. No coach thought I had what it takes. It made for a miserable athletic career.

Over the course of the next eight years of my basketball journey, I came to hate the very game that I had once fallen in love with.

However, when I officially hung up the sports shoes for VEJAs and traded a basketball for a microphone and a pen, I realized that all of this internal muck still needed to be dealt with. My unhealthy athletic mindset was now becoming an unhealthy ministry and familial mindset.

I needed help.

We are often much more of our past than we'd like to admit. Things that have been spoken over us, done to us, and said about us—for better or worse—stay with us. These are the "scripts" that tend to make up our internal dialogue.

Each of these scripts that we tend to latch onto permeates every part of our lives into adulthood. Looking back, I can trace my unforgiveness toward my AAU coach to a few different scripts.

Script #1: "I Must Be Perfect"

I grew up with good parents who had volatile fights. Especially in the years leading up to my dad's affair and parents' subsequent separation, shouting matches became routine in our household. Those moments were tense, difficult, and traumatic to endure. As the oldest of three at the time, I started to see myself as the peacekeeper of the house.

As long as I listen the first time, my mom won't get frustrated, which means she won't yell at my dad.

As long as I do what I'm supposed to, my dad won't get angry, which means he won't yell at my mom or brothers.

I remember, on multiple occasions, coming home and anticipating that one of my brothers was going to get in trouble. In an effort to keep the peace and avoid an explosion from my dad, I would proactively tell him what my brother had done wrong and offer a solution of how I would fix it. Perhaps that's where my orator skills came from.

I started to internalize their unhealth as my own, and it became my burden to carry.

Any sort of conflict or tension—to this day—immediately sends me into fix-it mode. Anxiety wells up within, and I often find myself longing for "flight" or, if I can't run, turning toward "fight" mode in order to defend my feelings. This is something that I'm still working through and processing in real time.

Being a pastor, I knowingly and (even more difficult) unknowingly fail, upset, and let down others daily. Over time I've become better at navigating these conversations and differentiating between my own ego and their (often) unrealistic expectations. But every now and then, I find myself in a fragile state where any conflict sends me into a panic to ensure that my "perfect" facade remains secure.

This doesn't help when another script that I've read over and over again in my life has been . . .

Script #2: "I'm Too Defensive"

"Freak out, MICAH!"

It was the fifth-grade lunch table. What do you expect?

Middle school is cruel to so many in so many ways. For me, middle school was where I was attached to the infamous nickname "Freak Out Micah." My friends Ben and David were arguing with me about religion. You know, just a stereotypical fifth grade conversation. However, Ben and David had said some hurtful things about Christianity that I took offense to. I started passionately defending my beliefs but eventually was shut down as they stopped debating and started yelling, "Freak out, MICAH!" over and over and over again.

The entire cafeteria grew quiet. I was so embarrassed. So ashamed.

And I began believing the script that I should never be passionate about anything, and anything that I *am* passionate about, I should second-guess.

Script #3: "I'm Not Good Enough"

Indiana basketball is different than basketball anywhere else. It just is. Indiana and basketball is like Texas and football. It's life here.

So, while living in Indiana during fifth and sixth grade, I found myself in competition with basically every boy in school to make my basketball team. Both years, I was placed on the B team. It was the second best out of the three teams (A, B, and C). And both years, it crushed me to my core. In middle school, there was a clear social hierarchy. Making and starring on the A team came with an immense amount of social capital. The guys on this team effectively ran the school. They were invited to all the hangouts, were crushed on by all the girls, and were supported and championed by all the parents, teachers, and administrators. Being on the B Team was a banishment to obscurity. For someone as image driven as I am, this was social annihilation.

The script that I began to believe was "you're not good enough." And most of my middle school years were spent chasing any way I could to fit in with the "in" crowd I so desperately wanted to belong to.

These three scripts concocted a scared, passive, compliant boy. The perfect people pleaser. I wanted to step on no toes, get in no trouble, and be accepted by everyone.

All of these scripts were already embedded in me when I made the eighth grade AAU team. It didn't matter that I had been held back a year, allowing me to be in the same grade as those my age. It didn't matter that I had grown six inches. It didn't matter that I had put in hours upon hours of work honing my skills.

I was a scared, passive, compliant boy who needed the affirmation and attention of a volunteer coach/dad. The weight of all my hurt and expectation was laid on this man.

The roots go deeper, however. I realized that my family tree is riddled with these scripts.

I've already shared that there's been extensive infidelity and lying on both sides of my family. Each set of grandparents had affairs and are divorced. All of my uncles and aunts have either been divorced or married someone who was. Divorce has even touched my immediate family. Extended family gatherings are typically centered on small talk or surface-level subjects. There is a lot of distance and division amid all the divorce.

For Rylei and me, the script was clear: divorce is inevitable. So, as we began our marriage, I reverted to that passive, scared, compliant boy in an effort not to rock the boat. *Well, as long as I don't do anything that makes her mad at me, we'll be fine.* In reality, it was a lazy way to love. And eventually, when I did make mistakes, I hid them, because I believed that conflict would cause separation.

Through all the infidelity in my family tree, I saw spouses who were told—explicitly or implicitly—"You're not good enough." That messaging had embedded itself within me. With so much hiddenness and lies weaved into my family tree, it was evident that truth and passion were not valued.

I got the hint.

Scripts like these have been present since the beginning of time. For instance, in the book of Genesis, the theme of lying can be traced down through Abraham's family line.

> Abraham lied (twice) about Sarah.[4]
>
> Rebekah helped Jacob lie to Issac.[5]
>
> Jacob's life was defined by lies—his name literally meant "deceiver."[6]
>
> Jacob's sons lied about Joseph's death after they sold him into slavery.[7]

Or how about the theme of sexual sin through the line of King David?

> David had at least eight wives and committed adultery with Bathsheba.[8]
>
> Solomon had seven hundred wives and three hundred concubines.[9]
>
> Rehoboam had eighteen wives and sixty concubines.[10]

These familial patterns extend not just negatively, but positively, like in the area of vocation. I myself am a second-generation pastor. My mom and dad blazed that trail for me growing up. My parents have also created a familial environment where asking for and receiving forgiveness has become commonplace. Our family highly values truth telling and authenticity. All traits that were fashioned out of pain and forged through years of healing. However, it's inevitable that parts of us—be it physical, mental, emotional, or our personality—are going to be passed down through our family line.

But it's also possible to break free from the cycle of sinful or destructive patterns. The story of Joseph rivets me because we see him reverse much of the brokenness that he was brought up in.[11]

Joseph—somehow, someway—was able to recognize the pain of jealousy, bitterness, and rage that his brothers carried, and he grieved immensely over their poor choices.[12]

And—somehow, someway—Joseph found the strength to forgive and reconcile with his brothers. He "reassured them and spoke kindly to them" as he provided for them and their children.[13]

My take? I think Joseph *learned* that strength.

Decades earlier, Joseph's father, Jacob, betrayed his uncle, Esau. It's a wild story of lying, deceit, and cunning manipulation that is dramatic enough that it could have its own episodic run on E! or MTV.[14]

For years, Jacob and Esau were estranged as Jacob went on to live the life Esau was supposed to live, having stolen his birthright. Over time, Jacob believed that all of Esau's resentment, anger, and subsequent thirst for revenge had steadily grown. And he knew that an encounter with his brother once again was inevitable.

That day comes, and Jacob sends messengers ahead of him to warn Esau of his impending arrival. The response? "We went to your brother Esau, and now he is coming to meet you, and four hundred men are with him."[15]

This doesn't seem like a welcome party to Jacob; it feels like a threat.

Oh no. Four hundred men?

He's coming to fight me.

He's coming for revenge.

He's coming to end my life.

All of these thoughts must have been zipping through Jacob's mind. So—cunning as he is (it runs in the family, remember?)—he devises a plan. He decides to pepper Esau's journey with waves and waves of gifts of livestock. His hope is that over time, Esau's temper will cool and be won over by Jacob's . . . ehrmmmm . . . generosity. Jacob's not being discreet about his plan whatsoever: "I will pacify him with these gifts I am sending on ahead; later, when I see him, perhaps he will receive me."[16]

The day arrives, and Jacob sees Esau with his party—all four hundred of them. This is the moment . . . Will Jacob's plan work?

Esau comes to meet him. Jacob walks ahead of his family and bows to the ground seven times. A sign of immense respect.

You have to wonder what is going through Jacob's mind while he bows, right? Is he waiting for Esau to come running, screaming, waving a sword to chop his brother's head off? Will Esau shoot an arrow through his heart while his eyes are to the ground? Will the four hundred men begin to encircle him?

Actually, none of that happens.

Instead, "Esau ran to meet Jacob and embraced him; he threw his arms around his neck and kissed him. And they wept."[17]

Stunning.

Rather than seek revenge, Esau seeks reconciliation. This is a forgiveness that can't be bought. Esau was able to work through the generational sin of his family's past.

He had grown up in a household of liars. His grandfather lied about being married to his grandmother.[18] His father lied about being married to his mother.[19] And his brother lied about being him.[20]

This was a pattern of failure that likely felt both unforgettable and unforgivable. And yet, Esau made a choice to break the generational sin of his past and to seek redemption rather than retribution, securing a future that looked vastly different from the one his family should have inherited.

This decision literally had generational effects.

Joseph's experience of suffering and God's kindness in the midst of it allowed him to differentiate between humanity's brokenness and God's goodness. Rather than blaming God for the terrible things that had happened to him, he was able to see God's kindness through the difficulties of life and forgive those who had wounded him.

But how? How did he learn to forgive such unforgettable offenses?

He watched his uncle do it.[21] That's right. Joseph was in the rear of Jacob's camp as his father bowed to the ground seven times, waiting to see how his uncle—who'd had everything stripped away from him by his brother—would respond. And it was a response of kindness, of forgiveness, of debt-release. This response allowed both Esau and Jacob to move forward in their lives.

Instead of allowing the roots of bitterness, cynicism, and anger to fester and grow, Joseph also released his perpetrators (his brothers) of their past sins. This allowed both Joseph and his brothers to move forward in their lives.

My friend, an invitation is offered to you and me to cut off our roots of bitterness, cynicism, and anger that are festering within and to release our perpetrators of past sins.

In place of hurt comes healing. In place of a destructive past and frustrating present comes a liberating future.

My eighth grade AAU coach carried the brunt of my cynicism, bitterness, and hatred for years. That continued to my high school and college coaches alike. Everyone was always out to get me. However, when I was able to examine my past, I realized I had placed these men on a voided pedestal I felt my fatherly lineage had created.

My dad had abandoned me.

My godfather had abandoned me.

My paternal grandfather had abandoned me.

My maternal grandfather had abandoned me.

The constant stream of abandonment by the men I admired most created a wound so deep that it began infecting every other area of my life.

"No one wants, cares for, appreciates, or loves me" was the script lodged into my soul. All of the hurt and pain was thrust upon my coaches. Playing time became a personal validation—or lack thereof—of worth, acceptance, and love. That event at Disney World was a microcosm of all the ways I felt unloved, unworthy, unaccepted, and overlooked by fatherly figures in my life.

The day things changed for me was when I collectively decided that I would forgive my forefather(s) for abandoning me. This was a yearslong process over many counseling sessions where I worked with tools like the genogram to uncover some of these familial patterns.[22] A genogram is simply a visual tool that allows you to name and notice relational patterns (good and bad) in your family tree up to three or four generations.

But there came a day when I noticed that something had shifted. I not only felt a release toward the father figures in my life but toward my coaches too. I recognized the ways that I had allowed bitterness and cynicism to creep into my heart, and I decided that I would forgive these men for the ways they had failed me—whether my expectations were reasonable or not. From that day on, I pledged to forge a new future, where my worth would be rooted first and foremost in Christ.

"I must be perfect," "I'm too defensive," and "I'm not good enough" all vanished as a new script of "I am chosen, holy, and dearly loved"[23] began to take root in my soul.

"We love because [God] first loved us."[24] We forgive because he first forgave us. There is nothing we have done that has earned the right to be forgiven. And there might be nothing that someone else has done to earn your forgiveness. But that's the rub. We don't deserve and we haven't earned forgiveness, but he gave it. And he expects us to freely give as we've freely received.

We fail to forgive when we brush away the invitation to come face-to-face with our hurt, our abusers, our accusers, and our wounds, and to choose another way forward.

This may seem impossible. But it's not. It's exactly what Jesus did.

God sent his one and only Son to this earth as an incarnate human baby. That baby grew up in a dysfunctional, complicated, messy family system just like you and me. He endured all of the pain, betrayal, abuse, and hurt of humanity's past, present, and future, and he unleashed forgiveness on *anyone* who chooses to receive it.

Not out of duty. Not out of force. Not out of coercion. Rather, out of love.

For you. And for me.

In response to that love, he invites us to love one another. To forgive so that we may be forgiven. Our ability to forgive is a testament to the God we serve. In a world drowning in the hurts of a sinful past, Jesus beckons us into a forgiving future.

The prophet Isaiah says it this way: "By his wounds we are healed."[25] The Wounded Healer is here. My friends, before us is a choice. To be bound by bitterness or to be freed by forgiveness.

I had to make a choice and decide if I was going to allow the actions of one man—magnified by the hurt of a multitude of men who had gone before me—plague me the rest of my life. Or, I had to decide if I was going to truly forgive him (them). And I realized that in letting go of that hurt and extending forgiveness, I was actually set free to be the real version of myself that God has called me to be.

As C. S. Lewis once wrote, "To be a Christian means to forgive the inexcusable, because God has forgiven the inexcusable in you. . . . But to forgive the incessant provocations of daily life . . . how can we do it? Only, I think, by remembering where we stand."[26]

Jesus is not asking us to simply forget the hurts of our past. Psychologically that is virtually impossible. But he is asking us to release and entrust the pain to him, the only one who could ever handle the weight of it all. That's the beauty of life with Jesus. There is a life awaiting you that is free of the burden that's weighing you down. A life where the roots of a poisoned family tree begin to recover and heal. Forgiveness is the key. It's been placed in your hand. Now it's up to you whether you will open the door and allow Jesus to enter.[27]

3

THE CYCLE OF FORGIVENESS

IT WAS AN OVERCAST SUMMER DAY. I was in the Chick-fil-A drive-through when I got the call. Parker was distraught.

"It's over. She's left me. We're done."

A few months earlier I had been on the phone with Parker, and all had seemed well in his marriage. Sure, there were some struggles and relational dynamics and practices that Rylei and I didn't agree with, but overall, it seemed to be a healthy first few years of marriage.

Two years earlier, Parker and his wife, Ellie, had moved states away. The physical distance created a relational distance that was difficult to navigate. Suddenly we weren't in each other's everyday lives like we used to be in college. There was an absence of context that was evident during this particular call.

"Wait, what? Parker, what is happening? What do you mean she's left? What do you mean you're done? What is going on?"

Just a year earlier, Rylei and I had visited them in their city that we loved. It was such a fun trip, and I remember thinking, *I really love it here, and I love that people I love are here.* Already, I was daydreaming of future backpacking trips, hikes, and visits to third-wave coffee shops with kids.

With one phone call, all of that came crashing down. I wasn't exactly sure what to say, so I just listened.

Ellie was once a chaplain on our Christian college campus. She has a vibrant, beautiful, smart, and witty personality. But as Parker began to tell me about their journey over the last year, I realized how much had been hidden regarding their situation.

Parker told me that for the last year, he and Ellie had been struggling with diverging outlooks in life. This divergence was identified early on in their relationship. However, it was a tension that had seemingly been put to rest as they dated, were engaged, and got married.

Over the course of time, Ellie began having doubts. And for a year, Parker carried the burden of those doubts alone on his shoulders. This was the day that all of those secrets would come to light.

As I pulled into a parking space to listen intently, I could feel the pain and hurt in Parker's voice. But there was also hope. Hope that reconciliation and restoration could still be possible. A desire to do whatever it took to save his marriage.

Within weeks, Parker and Ellie's immediate families were clued in on the severity of the situation—families that Rylei and I were and are extremely close to. It was painful to watch them navigate the complexity of everything. Ellie's feelings and internal wrestling was valid, but so was her love and covenantal pledge to Parker in marriage. It seemed like an almost unbearable tension. And eventually, that's exactly what it became.

Ellie desired more and more a different way of life—one that did not include being married to Parker. It was a tragic situation to walk through. To watch two people you love end a marriage is gut-wrenching. However, I wasn't prepared for the anger that would rise to the surface of my soul in defense of the person I believed to have been wronged.

In my righteous anger, I wanted to call Ellie. I wanted to debate and contest her decision. I wanted justice—or at least, what I *thought* was justice.

Truthfully, I just wanted to see Parker and Ellie flourish. God's design is for human flourishing. And I believe the way of Jesus is the road map to discovering such a life. I didn't think the way Ellie was choosing to move forward would lead to that.

What made the situation more complex was that—at this point in time—Parker and Ellie had both renounced Christianity. So even if I did have the chance to argue or debate with her, we would have approached the situation from two completely different playing fields.

And so, after much prayer and deliberation, Rylei and I concluded that the best way to love them would not be to thump them over the head with a Bible, debate theology, offer research, or engage in skillful debate with persuasive facts or statistics. Rather, we decided the best way to love these people we desperately care about would be to pray for them, to offer support when called upon, to speak only when invited to, and to fall in line behind Parker and follow his lead with respect to moving forward in his marriage.

It's been three years since that conversation took place in the Chick-fil-A parking lot, and I wish that there was a "happy" ending to share. Parker and Ellie sought counsel and wrestled through the implications of their decision. There's been a lot of pain, a lot of anger, and a lot of questioning that has taken place. Parker and Ellie are now divorced. She stayed put, and Parker went back home to live with his family. Relationships have been strained or outright ended—not out of bitterness or resentment but simply due to a lack of relational proximity. All of this grieves me.

But, in the midst of this complex, hurtful, difficult situation, I have watched Parker live out the process of forgiving Ellie in an intimately familiar and Christlike way.

My mom wrote in her memoir after watching her husband walk out on her with a mistress, "Forgiveness is only true forgiveness when you forgive regardless of the person's response. Grace is unmerited favor, a gift offered with no strings attached. Forgiveness is a gift that flows from grace. In forgiveness, we give up our right to throw our stones in retaliation for the hurt the other has caused us."[1]

That pretty much summarizes how I've watched Parker process watching his spouse walk away from their marriage. Parker didn't intend for his marriage to dissolve two years in. He didn't plan for his wife to choose a life that would not include being married to him. He didn't expect life to look the way that it does. And yet, at every turn, when I wanted to throw stones, I watched Parker set his down. He has taught me so much about what it looks like to preserve relationship in love, to express anger healthily, to offer truth kindly, and to press forward hopefully.

Over the course of time, I've found Parker pastoring me away from anger and into empathy. Away from rage and into patience. There's still a great deal he and I disagree upon theologically and ideologically, but he's taught me a lot about what it looks like to love and forgive someone who has deeply wounded you.

It has been this tension that has actually brought him back around to considering Jesus as Lord. Through the process of his divorce, he's begun to discover a God who is both righteous and compassionate to forgive.

The tension of righteous standards and perfect love is the paradigm by which followers of Jesus enter into a process of forgiving one another. It is not less than righteousness and it is not less than compassionate forgiveness; it is both. But there does seem to be a pattern.

For instance, in Exodus 34, Moses is on Mount Sinai conversing with God. The Scriptures say that God passed by Moses in the form of a cloud and said, "The LORD, the LORD, the compassionate and gracious God, slow to anger, abounding in love and faithfulness, maintaining love to thousands, and forgiving wickedness, rebellion and sin. Yet he does not leave the guilty unpunished; he punishes the children and their children for the sin of the parents to the third and fourth generation."[2]

Do you see it?

Forgiveness and accountability.

Righteousness and compassion.

Mercy, mercy, mercy, with justice in tow.

If you're in need of care, God is compassionate and gracious. If you've messed up, God is slow to anger. If you need love, God is abounding in it. If you've been betrayed, God is faithful. If you need forgiveness, he forgives you. If you need to forgive someone else, he empowers you.

But . . . if you need justice, God is just. He does not leave the guilty unpunished. The invitation is for us to forgive, to allow God to heal and restore, and to trust that in the end, justice will prevail.

We serve a God who is both/and, my friends. He's holy *and* kind, patient *and* powerful. He judges accordingly and demonstrates accountability, but it is all filtered through the lens of the Cross. Through the lens of love, redemption, relationship, and reconciliation. Through forgiveness.

Or how about God's words to the prophet Micah? God reduces the 613 commandments that the Israelites were expected to uphold down to three. Three simple commands. And what are those three commands?

"He has shown you, O mortal, what is good. And what does the LORD require of you? To act justly and to love mercy and to walk humbly with your God."[3] Ah . . . justice, mercy, humility. In other words, forgiveness does not require the abandonment of conviction. We are to uphold what is good, true, and beautiful. In fact, that may be the most compassionate thing we can do in the process of forgiving someone.

This is what Jesus does for all of us. He does not expose us in a humiliating way. He's not seeking to "catch" you. He's seeking to pursue and hold you. God's righteous nature is revealing in a gentle, honest, authentic, invitational way. It's the heart-wrenching question "Where are you?"[4] He's beckoning us to step out of the dark and into the light so that we can be and become people of grace as he, in fact, shows grace to us. We grow in our capacity to forgive when we remember how much we have been forgiven.

When our spouse does something that upsets or annoys us, forgive.

When our coworker does something that hurts or embarrasses us, forgive.

When our hero has a public, moral failure, forgive.

None of this is done in an effort to let people "get away" with sin. We're not letting people off the hook. Consequences are justified and should be exercised. But our heart posture toward the offender should be one of mercy. We are to forgive others, as we have been forgiven ourselves.

Jesus, in the Lord's Prayer, is to the point with his words: "And forgive us our debts, as we also have forgiven our debtors. . . . For if you forgive other people when they sin against you, your heavenly Father will also forgive you. But if you do not forgive others their sins, your Father will not forgive your sins."[5]

Notice how all of this is tied together. The level of forgiveness we receive is intimately connected to the level of forgiveness we offer. Justice and mercy are held in tension through humility. It is not our job to judge others. Should we place ourselves in the position of God, we will have to live up to the standard of God.[6]

So, instead, we pursue humility. Humility comes through repentance. I grew up with Hannah Montana belting, "Everyone makes mistakes."[7] A 2000s cringe, pop, Disney echo of a similar refrain from the apostle Paul.[8] This truth properly positions us to navigate the complex relational waters of forgiveness.

How about Jesus in Matthew 5? This passage is sure to make those of us struggling to forgive another person squirm: "Blessed are the merciful, for they will be shown mercy. . . . Blessed are the peacemakers, for they will be called children of God."[9]

My friend, these are not half-hearted or thrown-together statements of Jesus. There's no qualifier. He does not say, "Blessed—maybe—are the merciful." Or "Blessed—if I feel like it—are the merciful." Or "Blessed—sometimes—are the peacemakers."

It's pretty straightforward. "Blessed are the merciful, for they will be shown mercy." "Blessed are the peacemakers, for they will be called children of God." Give, receive. Offer, take. Show, shown. Forgive, forgiven. This is who our God is!

But so often, our own fallen, fallible, human hearts scream on the inside, "THAT ISN'T FAIR." In case all of this is upsetting you, please hear me: you're right—*none* of it's fair.

You . . . me . . . we(!) don't deserve it. We haven't earned it. We certainly aren't owed it. And yet, therein lies the beauty of the gospel. None of us want to see our enemies or those who hurt us be forgiven, but to withhold forgiveness from others means to withhold it from ourselves. Because "all have sinned and fall short of the glory of God."[10]

Jesus—with an immense amount of kindness, but full of truth and justice—declared this statement unconditionally. It's a matter of fact. Show compassion, receive compassion.

Now, please know, this isn't a get out of jail free card. Bad choices beget bad consequences. Sinful decisions reap destruction, pain, and loss. However, if forgiveness and reconciliation are pursued, then sin or evil never has the last word. It is always, continually, eternally written over, *eleēmōn*, *eleēmōn*, *eleēmōn*.

Mercy, mercy, mercy . . . with justice in tow. Forgiving as we have been forgiven.

So, how do we go about forgiving people who've wounded us?

As I've walked this out with Parker and Ellie, I've seen the consequences of the decision that Ellie made. And yet, in the midst of that, I witnessed Parker extend grace as he tenderly, patiently navigated those hurdles with Ellie. It would have been easy for him to brashly demand a quick and easy settlement, but he chose the harder road of keeping communication channels open.

In my own processing, I've had to wrestle through the tension between righteousness and compassion with Ellie's decision. On the one hand, in my humanity, I've wanted consequences to be felt, pain to be endured, and regret to be experienced. But, over the years, as I've watched Parker navigate his own journey with immense grace, it has gradually softened my heart toward Ellie. While I grieve that what was is no longer, I also have developed a deeper level of love and care for her. In order to respect her boundaries, we've decided not to initiate contact. However, I've come to a place in my own journey of forgiveness that if she called today in need, I would stop what I was doing in order to help her.

Getting to this place often takes time. Usually (not always) the deeper the hurt, the longer it takes. Forgiving someone—like being forgiven—is both a practice and a process. The practice of forgiveness is just that . . . a practice. It is something we do. It is a conscious decision we make. It is acknowledging a debt that is owed and making the determination to wipe the ledger clean.

Forgiving as practice is pretty straightforward. It is making a decision inwardly and expressing that decision outwardly by communicating the words "I forgive you." Essentially, you're telling that person, "In this moment, I am releasing you from the debt that you have incurred." Sometimes we consciously decide to forgive but then must process those feelings over time. Or we might process our hurt first.

The other night, I said something that hurt Rylei's feelings. After she named it, I grew defensive, which only hurt her more. Instead of seeing how my words had negatively affected her, I doubled down in pride. When I finally did come around to apologize, I asked, "Will you forgive me?" And her answer was honest: "Not yet." She wasn't withholding forgiveness from me. She was processing the hurt that had taken place and wanted to ensure that she could—with integrity—release me from the debt. Before she could practice forgiveness, she needed to process forgiveness (more on that in a moment). Later that night, I circled back around and asked, "Will you forgive me?" At that point, she was ready. She said, "I forgive you." A conscious decision had been made and was communicated verbally. What had been fractured in our relationship earlier in the night was now on the mend.

See, the practice of forgiveness often does not remove the pain of the initial problem. Which is why we must turn now to forgiving as process.

There is a process to forgiving. And this process is cyclical. Forgiving and working through hurt can happen simultaneously, as an ongoing practice (and therefore, as an ongoing process). In my opinion, the greater the wound, the more times around the forgiving cycle is required. As author and pastor Peter Scazzero notes, "Forgiveness is not a quick process. I do not believe it is possible to truly forgive another person from the heart until we allow ourselves to feel the pain of what was lost."[11]

With that in mind, let's look at forgiving as process.

1. Grieve

The first step is to grieve. We must acknowledge the injustice that has been done. Whether small or big, we have to face that the hurt we feel has been directed toward us. To miss this crucial step allows denial to creep in. And when denial creeps in, we are unable to see clearly. The sooner we can acknowledge the hurt that's been done, face it, and grieve it, the sooner we can heal.

Dr. Jerry L. Sittser is a professor, theologian, and scholar at Whitworth University. Among his most influential books written is one entitled *A Grace Disguised: How the Soul Grows through Loss*. In it, Jerry vulnerably shares about the tragic car accident that took the lives of his mother, wife, and young daughter. After more than thirty years since that awful incident, Jerry reflected, "The secret [of grief] is to carry the past in a way that is redemptive. . . . Mourning should be a part of a Christian lifestyle. Our capacity to mourn should grow as we become mature Christians."[12] David writes in Psalm 34, "The LORD is close to the brokenhearted and saves those who are crushed in spirit."[13]

A few years back, I went through a painful situation with an overseer of mine. The man I thought I was working for turned out to be living a double life, hiding an addiction, even as he pastored me through my own. I felt disoriented and unsure of what was real. I decided I needed to take a step back from our relationship in order to grieve. This was a man I had trusted with intimate details of my life, deep dreams in my soul, and situations that I was walking through personally. The relationship we once had was beautiful in many ways, but it was also built on a lie. This was someone who was supposed to protect me and shepherd me who ended up causing great hurt. I've had to mourn that I may never have that relationship with him again.

My friend, if you find yourself in a state of grief right now, that does not make you wrong or bad. A failure to grieve will hold you captive in a prison of offense, and authentic forgiveness and true freedom will always elude you. We must grieve past pain in order to appreciate present grace and inherit future blessing.

2. Reassess

After we grieve, we must reassess and take inventory of what comes next. Are there new boundaries that must be drawn with the person who hurt you? Are there natural consequences that need to be communicated to them, either by you or a trusted third party? Are there practices that need to be put in place for your protection moving forward?

That could mean putting physical distance between you, a change of scenery, or a fresh start altogether. Maybe you need to limit the amount of contact you have with that person going forward. Not because you haven't forgiven them, but because a lack of boundaries would insinuate that their mishandling of your relationship equates to no consequences.

Eventually, I reestablished contact with my overseer, and I found our relationship continuing with the same level of access as before. As I reassessed, I realized that I needed to set a communication boundary limiting access to the details of my day-to-day life. The consequences of his actions meant that we no longer had relational (or physical) proximity to one another as his family moved for the sake of their healing process. And in order to protect my own heart, I needed to live into that new reality rather than pretend that nothing had changed.

In the process of forgiving someone, grace and space are imperative. You owe it to yourself to create some distance between yourself and the person who hurt you—to the degree that is appropriate. This need not be an eternal change. But it is a necessary one.

3. Build

Reassessment is an ongoing, fluid step in the process of forgiving someone. At some point, the relationship that has been deconstructed can and should be reconstructed into whatever its next iteration is going to be.[14]

Jesus longs for us to rebuild toward wholeness, restoration, and reconciliation.

However, this takes time. And over time, trust must be earned back. With right action comes right authority and influence.

This is presently the stage I'm at with my overseer. It has been almost two years, and we've sat down for coffee a few times. I've had to be diligent about guarding my heart to ensure I'm not oversharing. Trust has been lost. It can be earned back, but it takes time.

The disciples eventually understood this. At some point, Jesus had reassessed where his disciples were spiritually and felt the time was right to leave this world and impart his Holy Spirit. They then went out to preach the good news of the gospel to all. This coming of the Holy Spirit gave the disciples a power, intimacy, and faith that they had yet to experience prior to Jesus' ascension. This reassessment eventually led to an even further intimacy of relationship than before. When we rebuild, restoration and resurrection is made possible.

Even when the healing words "I forgive you" have been initially spoken, that does not mean that "I trust you" is a given. Forgiveness does not equal an immediate restoration of trust. Forgiveness may be instant. Trust and healing take time.

So give the person you've forgiven time to prove that they've truly repented—that they desire to go a different route, to live a different way. Give them time to show you that their character is changing for the better. Give them space to build and grow other healthy relationships in their life that don't involve you.

If they lied, give them time to prove they're a truth-teller.

If they cheated, give them time to prove they're faithful.

If they were unkind to you, give them time to prove their heart is softening.

Forgiveness doesn't mean forgetfulness. But it also doesn't mean bondage. It shouldn't be held over the offender like a carrot dangled on a stick. Instead, in your reassessment, offer ways that trust can be earned and restoration can take place.

True, authentic forgiveness begins with a heart posture that desires reconciliation and restoration. This doesn't mean that trust will ever fully be earned back. But it does mean loving and living with a desire and hopefulness that it can.

When my parents were separated, my dad—after resigning and relinquishing his qualification for the pastorate—had to get another job in order to provide some sort of income for our family even though he wasn't living with us. He had to come fully clean in counseling about the sins of his past and the hiddenness he was tightly clinging to. His provision for our family was a demonstration of his desire for reconciliation. He was backing up his words with actions. And so, the dinner shift at P. F. Chang's as a waiter became the new normal.

When I reflect on that season of life, I look back with a profound amount of respect for my dad. This was a man who was a highly public figure, rocking a white button-down and black apron, serving food to people he used to preach to. I imagine it was humiliating and humbling. And yet, I never once saw my dad complain or excuse or defend. He understood the consequences of his actions and was willing to do whatever he could to rectify his relationship with his wife and kids. Eventually, Dad would return home, but only after months of intense, crucial repair had taken place.

In 1 Corinthians 5, we see Paul handling a case of local church discipline. A man is sleeping with his father's wife. The man's lack of repentance for such an egregious act carries with it the consequence of excommunication from his church family. He is cut off. That is the result of failing to admit that what he's engaging in is wrong. However, this man eventually repents. He does acknowledge that what he's done is sinful.

So, in Paul's second letter to the Corinthians, he instructs the church to restore the man back into the community.[15] Bad choices beget bad consequences. But good choices, made consistently over time, beget good consequences. In the realm of the here and now, the stakes are high. But in the realm of eternity, the stakes are even higher. Eternal life hinges on making the choice to acknowledge Jesus as Lord and Savior. To pledge allegiance to him as King. And to recognize him as the way, the truth, and the life—as the only pathway to reconciliation with the Father.

When true repentance is shown and there is a desire to change, restoration should be the end goal in the cycle of forgiving someone.

Please note, again, *this takes time*. Please don't misread me as telling you that at the first sign of repentance, full restoration should take place. Again, the bigger the offense, the longer amount of time it often takes to heal and restore trust. Forgiveness is not a license to forget. Forgiveness is mercy, mercy, mercy . . . with justice in tow. This is the cycle of forgiveness. This is forgiving as process.

PART II

ASKING

FOR

FORGIVENESS

4

TRANSFORMED ASSUMPTIONS

OUR LIVES HAVE BEEN SHAPED by assumptions.

Now, this isn't entirely a bad thing. Assumptions play a crucial role in everyday survival. They fill in the gaps of what we think and perceive, helping us make sense of our complex world. The problem isn't that we make assumptions; it's that we assume too much.

We assume that because a person lied to us once, they will always lie to us and can never be trusted again. We assume that because someone made an offhand comment here, they're just a jerk everywhere. We assume that because she yelled at her kid, she's a bad parent.

The problem isn't that we make assumptions; it's that we assume too much.

We can't redeem past hurts, pains, and failures if we are not open to reframing our assumptions about others' motives or the grace that is available to them and us. We can't realize our own failings and our need to ask for forgiveness unless we examine the assumptions we make.

I am not saying that we should trust someone who has perpetually lied to us. I am saying that we should be people of second chances. We should be people who assume the best until proven otherwise. And we should seek to be people of grace, love, and understanding in our relationships.

You can't move forward in forgiveness if you're unwilling to release the self-made narratives of your past. Your hurt is valid, your pain is justified, but your resentment is holding you back from embracing the future God desperately wants you to step into. Forgiveness starts from a posture of humble curiosity.

Often our assumptions become the primary barrier to experiencing transformation and healing. We can't be curious about something or someone that we've already come to a conclusion on.

As followers of Jesus, we must embrace another way. A way not of cynicism but of curiosity. A way not of assumption but of wonder.

"I am so, so sorry. I was completely wrong."

These are the words that I shamefully spoke over a phone call as I confessed my ignorance to a person I had deeply hurt.

It was a spring day, still in the early stages of team building for The Sanctuary—a church we planted inside the loop of Indianapolis. Our community was small, but we were tight. We were young but passionate. On this particular day, that passion, fueled by a multitude of assumptions, gave way to a host of pain.

I remember where I was standing when I sent the original text with (what I believed to be) righteous anger coursing through my veins. A team member had posted something online that I thought was inappropriate and contradictory to a conversation we'd had a few days prior. Even if my tone was gentle—"pastoral"—a simple read between the lines communicated much more. I was frustrated, and I had trouble hiding it.

Then, the reply came: "Everything you just said is completely off base. Here's what really happened." As she explained the situation, it turned out, she was right. There was a lot of context surrounding her post that actually made the content completely appropriate and understandable.

But the damage had been done. I had assumed a great deal. And you know what they say about assuming?

Well, I'll let you finish that one.

―――

Assumptions can have generational repercussions. Scientists have discovered that we—as human beings—can be conditioned to believe anything through repetition. They call this the illusory truth effect.[1]

This is why you believe that if you swallow gum, it takes seven years to digest in your stomach. Why you believe that we only use 10 percent of our brains. Why every two-year-old is immediately met with suspicion on the day of their birthday as they enter the dreaded "terrible twos." It's why you believe that cracking your knuckles leads to arthritis. And why boys everywhere are shaving the three hairs on their chest and chin, believing the hair will grow back faster and thicker.

We've assumed these things to be true because they're what we've been told. These are stories that have been repeated. We—as human beings—are story-wired. We make sense of life through story. Think about it: the Scriptures are a multitude of stories within a larger story. The Bible as a whole is simply one great story—typically broken down into four parts: Creation, Fall,

Redemption, and Restoration. There is a clear narrative arc to the Scriptures—and to life.

All of life is filtered through story.

When we meet a new person, we ask, "What's your story?" When we visit new places, we are attracted to museums and landmarks that tell the story of that particular destination. Common entertainment like movies, TV, or books hook us through the use of story.

Story is how we make sense of the world around us. For all of human history, civilization has passed down stories from generation to generation, preserving the context of where we came from and how we got here. The problem isn't inherently with the stories we tell. It's with the stories we believe. The Scriptures are not withheld.

At a broad level, many believe that the Bible was originally written in English because it's so widely distributed in English. But the Bible was actually written in Hebrew, Aramaic, and Greek. Others assume that the Bible is a book. In actuality, it is a portable library containing sixty-six different books.

At a more cultural level, many assume Jesus was a fair-skinned hippie simply because that is how he is portrayed in so many works of medieval art and literature. In reality, he was born and descended from a Middle Eastern society. This pegs him to look much more like someone from Bethlehem than Boise.

Or there's the assumption that every word in the Bible is supposed to be read literally. This interpretation has done great damage throughout Christian history. The Bible—in totality—is to be read *literarily*, not necessarily literally. There are different genres, themes, and motifs that proper readership of the text draws out, revealing the full picture of Scripture and its consistent declaration—that Jesus the Son is Lord who was sent by God the Father to rescue and redeem humanity in order to usher in a new heaven and earth for all of eternity.

More specifically, assumptions are made about individual stories in the Bible. Many people assume that Noah's ark was filled with two (a pair) of every kind of animal. A closer reading shows that there were actually *seven* twos (pairs) of every kind of clean animal.[2] That's fourteen for those not counting.

Or how about Jesus calming the storm with his disciples in a boat? Most of us assume that it's only Jesus and his pals out on that great, big lake. Except it's not. The Gospel writer Mark notes, "Leaving the crowd behind, they took him along, just as he was, in the boat. *There were also other boats with him.*"[3]

Now hear me out: your interpretation of Scripture often comes with many assumptions—some helpful, some not so much. Life also comes with many assumptions. Perhaps you find yourself turning these pages while simultaneously dealing with the fallout of those assumptions.

Perhaps you're reading these words while trying to put back together the pieces of a life that doesn't look how you assumed it would. Maybe you're trying to discern how something so bad could have happened to someone so good. Or you're trying to figure out why the outcome you thought you could control never materialized.

In the pain of your reality, you've been left feeling disoriented and distracted with thoughts—assumptions—like these:

Life has not given me what it owes me. This is not what I deserve.

I'm probably being punished by God for my lack of obedience toward him.

God clearly doesn't care about me because of what I've had to endure.

The person who hurt me is never going to be held accountable for what they've done. They'll forever get away with it.

The person I've hurt is never going to forgive me. It's too late to ask for forgiveness.

Forgiveness isn't available to them.

Forgiveness isn't available to me.

These assumptions—whether explicitly on the surface of our lives or implicitly in the crevices of our hearts—are shaping and forming who we're becoming. People of bitterness rather than grace. People of revenge rather than reconciliation. People of cynicism rather than forgiveness.

We must understand how ingrained certain sets of assumptions are within us. Then, if we're going to allow God to redeem a past full of failures (either ours or others') and secure a future of forgiveness and reconciliation, we have to be willing to let God *transform* our assumptions.

Your assumptions will not go away. As previously mentioned, the problem isn't *that* we assume, it's more *what* we assume. We have to be willing to open our closed-off hearts and made-up minds; we have to be willing to risk being hurt, let down, disappointed, or betrayed for the reward of experiencing intimacy with others and with Christ. We have to be willing to admit where we were wrong and then ask for, receive, and freely give grace.

The Good News of Jesus is that when we pledge our allegiance to him as Lord, we are adopted into a relationship with a Person who never fails, never lets us down, and never disappoints. Who has forgiven our failures eternally. This is not to say that there are not frustrating, confusing, or painful aspects to life with God (we'll get to that in part 4). But it is to say that much of our disappointment stems not from a lack of care or love on God's part but a lack of understanding or insight on ours.

There is a humility of heart required to become the type of person who is willing to embrace failure and ask for forgiveness. Who lives by the often-backward values of the Kingdom of Heaven.

It is to a few of those values that we now turn . . .

In Matthew chapter 20, Jesus, being the master Jedi[4]—I mean teacher—that he is, offers a fascinating word picture of what transformed assumptions look like.

The story goes that "the kingdom of heaven is like a landowner who went out early in the morning to hire workers for his vineyard. He agreed to pay them a denarius [day's wages] for the day and sent them into his vineyard."[5]

A pretty straightforward exchange, yeah?

So, Jesus continues the story. He explains that throughout the day—9 a.m., 12 p.m., 3 p.m., 5 p.m.—the landowner is out walking in the marketplace and finds laborers without work. He says to them, "'You also go and work in my vineyard, and I will pay you whatever is right.' So they went."[6]

By the end of the day, this landowner has a whole team of laborers working in his vineyard. A lot is happening on this plot of land. The end of the shift comes, and the owner of the vineyard summons all the workers, beginning with those who were hired last and finishing with those who were hired first.

Jesus says,

> The workers who were hired about five in the afternoon came and each received a denarius. So when those came who were hired first, they expected to receive more. But each one of them also received a denarius. When they received it, they began to grumble against the landowner. "These who were hired last worked only one hour," they said, "and you have made them equal to us who have borne the burden of the work and the heat of the day." But he answered one of them, "I am not being unfair to you, friend. Didn't you agree to work for a denarius? Take your pay and go. I want to give the one who was hired last the same as I gave you. Don't I have the right to do what I want with my own money? Or are you envious because I am generous?" So the last will be first, and the first will be last.[7]

Woof.

Not the ending you'd expect, right?

To recap, here we have a simple exchange: one day's work for one day's pay. All is well. But then workers start showing up later and later before, eventually, getting paid out the same as those who started in the morning and had to endure the Middle Eastern heat.

Where's the fairness in that?

Do you see it? Their assumptions getting turned upside down? The men assumed. Actually, the Scriptures note, they "expected." In Greek, it's this word *enomisan*, and it literally means "to suppose."[8] These men logically connected the dots to an outcome they were hoping for. Instead, what seemed to be a generous and favorable offer to the later workers ended up being a fair offer to the earlier workers as well.

But that's the point.

Jesus notes that the landowner was not being unfair. He paid the men what they had agreed to be paid. There was no harm done and no promise broken.

And yet . . . it didn't seem fair.

This is the great tragedy of assumptions. We tend to insert ourselves into the story where God belongs in an attempt to usurp his authority. We believe that we're the landowner, but we're not. We're the workers.

One of my favorite quotes is by a pastor named John Ortberg, who gently admonishes, "There is a God, and you aren't him."[9] That's what Jesus is saying here. He's saying, "Hey, if you really want to put yourself in the role of God, understand that there will be a requirement from God."

Jesus is crystal clear: "If you forgive other people when they sin against you, your heavenly Father will also forgive you. But if you do not forgive others their sins, your Father will not forgive your sins."[10]

Unforgiveness comes with conditions. If you hold to unforgiveness, then you won't be forgiven. If we are to forgive others, then it should be to the same degree we ourselves would like to be forgiven. To get to a position where we can forgive others, we first have to see clearly how we've fallen short and ask for forgiveness for those areas. Only then are we able to give others the same grace that we've already received. And this is where we—in our cultural moment—have drifted so drastically.

Rather than holding people accountable after examining our own assumptions, we instead hold bitterness and resentment toward others and have created a culture where failure is final and personal opinions reign supreme.

Jesus seems to be playing by a different set of rules. And the most frustrating part about this is that he is under no obligation to make sense of his ways for us. Sure, he offers us pieces. Stories of virtues that seem to contradict the values of this world but— according to Jesus—lead to flourishing. Paradoxes like these:

Losing your life to save it.[11]

Taking on the lowest position (that of a servant) to become great.[12]

Being last to be first.[13]

And yes, examining ourselves before calling out others.[14]

None of these principles seem sensical. Especially in a culture where self-preservation, celebrity status, wealth, and elitism are valued, right?

Exactly.

We've reached the crux of the issue. Notice the landowner's rebuke: "Don't I have the right to do what I want with my own money? Or are you envious because I am generous?"[15]

The landowner is not challenging the workers' rationale; he's challenging their resentment.

So often, our assumptions hinder our journey toward maturity, asking for forgiveness, and desiring reconciliation because we've refused to allow the pain of our past to be transformed. Instead, our pain is being transferred into our present and future.

"There is a God, and you aren't him." This is a stark but powerful truth. One that rightsizes our assumptions in view of God's mercy. How are we to explain his compassion? In some ways, we can't. It's upside down. It's backward. It's nonsensical. But it is right, good, and true. Because it is enveloped in his character.

The phrase Jesus uses in verse 15 in place of "envious" is this term *ponēros*,[16] which means "evil eye." This was a popular phrase that Jesus' audience would've been familiar with. It denotes a spirit of envy and jealousy. It literally means "to covet." We desire what someone else has, and this covetousness inhibits us from moving on from past hurts or what we perceive to be injustices. It prevents us from asking for forgiveness—because we assume that we don't have a need for it. It places all the blame on someone else and keeps us from seeking healing.

As I've worked through some of the pain in my own life, I've used three questions to sort through what hurts need to be addressed (either via counseling, a direct conversation, or wise counsel from others) and what needs to be transformed within me by God.

Once again, I don't know your story. There may be a great deal of legitimate pain, hurt, and injustice that you've endured. But I'm also sure there is a great deal of legitimate pain, hurt, and injustice that has become illegitimate resentment, jealousy, and bitterness.

All of these emotions can be fueled by assumptions. To discern this distinction, here are the three questions I ask.

1. What needs reflection?
Whenever I find myself ruminating on past hurt, I ask the question, "What do I need to reflect deeper on?" Perhaps I misread a motive in someone's actions. Maybe I misinterpreted a word they said or the tone of voice they used. Maybe I contributed to the conflict and

need forgiveness too. I try to replay the scene in my mind over and over again, looking for ways that Satan may have been using one of his most deadly, deceptive tactics—lying—to make me believe something untrue.

As we reflect on past hurt or pain, I believe that we—through the power of the Holy Spirit, in addition to (if necessary) supportive community or wise counsel—are able to discern what's justice-oriented and what's jealous-oriented.

2. What needs to be rewired?

In this reflection period, I then pray the prayer of David: "Search me, God, and know my heart; test me and know my anxious thoughts. See if there is any offensive way in me, and lead me in the way everlasting."[17]

It is in these moments, as I've reflected on events of past hurt, that I start to notice ugly aspects of my own heart that contributed to the situation. In my case, it's often ego, selfish ambition, and a desire to please people, or to appear better than I am—more successful, competent, and intelligent.

Here, I ask God, "What needs to be rewired? What assumptions from past experiences do you need to transform so that I don't transfer those assumptions into present or future relationships?" I'm often surprised and humbled at the gracious ways God illuminates these insights to me.

This rewiring becomes the crucible of transformation in the healing process. We can't become people of forgiveness if we're not willing to first recognize the mercy we need and ask for it.

3. What is required?

Finally, I ask Jesus, "What is now required of me? Where do I go from here?"

Jesus' concluding line in Matthew 20 may feel like a bit of an ominous cliff-hanger: "So the last will be first, and the first will be last."[18]

Really? That's it? But that's the point. Jesus leaves his audience with the antidote to assumption. Wonder.

Wonder is all around us, just waiting to be discovered. This can only happen when we trade in assumption for attention. It is from this position of humility that we realize we also need grace.

I've had to work through this paradigm multiple times as a local church planter the last few years. When I look back on my journey, there are a few specific moments that rise to the surface that—to this day—are still painful to reflect on. First, I can remember being told by a leader I greatly respect that the model of church leadership I felt was imperative to begin with would not work. Another painful moment came during a phone call with a pastor—again, someone I deeply respect and admire—who told me that their church would not be supporting our church plant. One final memory was not anything that happened directly to me but instead, things that were happening around me at the time—the rapid, exponential growth of friends' churches at a size and scale we couldn't match.

In all three instances, what was required was *wonder*. I had to take a step back to examine my own attitudes and motivations. Then I needed my assumptions to not just be released but transformed. And over time, I've seen that shift take place.

In this time of rewiring, I learned that what was required was recapturing the wonder of church planting in the first place. I didn't step out to copy and paste an older generation of pastor's leadership strategy—successful as it might be. I didn't sign up for this assignment to achieve a certain level of security, celebrity, fame, or renown. I didn't sign up to plant The Sanctuary so that it would be X number of people big or even so we'd see X number of people come to faith. I planted the church out of sheer obedience and faithfulness to the calling that God had placed on my life. Full stop. This perspective shift has allowed me to appreciate all the beautiful things God has done throughout the life of our church.

After twenty-four no's, we received a wonderful yes on our first facility as a church, a beautiful art center right in the cultural epicenter of Indianapolis's north side. We received financial provision not from one megachurch with mega resources but from hundreds of individuals, couples, families, and churches that tangibly showed the power of the generous family of God on full display.

We have seen a community—that started from nothing—in a part of town where the church has often been on its heels, not just grow but thrive. I've come to appreciate all these things simply by allowing my assumptions to be transformed from worry and insecurity into wonder and trust. It turns out, I was the one who needed to ask for a change in perspective.

The problem isn't that we assume; it's that we assume incorrectly. Many of us are daily dealing with false beliefs that build a bedrock of bitterness, hurt, and resentment for our lives to fragilely stand on.

I now assume that God will be faithful. I now assume that God is using encouragement and admonishment for the health of my soul and leadership. I now assume that God will build his church. I now assume that God will provide. I now assume that God is bigger than my preferences, convictions, and desires.

All of these assumptions are the result of transformation through the hard work of reflection, rewiring, and naming what's required moving forward. This transformation has allowed me to forgive the hurt, pain, and jealousy that I've experienced over the years—and to ask for forgiveness for the hurt I've caused.

We must pay attention. We must slow ourselves down long enough to process our past so that the still, small voice of God can lovingly transform our prior assumptions into present attention.

When we learn to pay attention, wonder becomes a healing balm that makes us soft and sensitive toward those around us. We start to love more like Jesus.

We lead from a place of curiosity rather than cynicism. We operate from a place of generous offering rather than greedy hoarding. We trust the Landowner rather than seeking explanation.

My friend, learn to pay attention.

Pay attention to your past. Pay attention to your shortcomings and faults. Pay attention to the humanity of the person you're interacting with. Pay attention to the beauty—faults and all—of the person you get to love.

Pay attention to the beauty that surrounds you. Pay attention and watch how God moves unexpectedly, unashamedly, and unimpededly as King. But also pay attention and watch how God moves subtly, mysteriously, and miraculously through people—everyday, ordinary people. Ostracized and marginalized people. Forgotten and abandoned people. The Kingdom of God unfolds around us here and now. Those who lose their life find it. Those who serve become great. Those who come last go first.

Can I gently encourage you today? Look up.

As painful as your past may have been, Jesus is inviting you to fix your eyes on him.

It's not fair that your coworker got the promotion, and you didn't. It's not fair that they had a great childhood, and you didn't. It's not fair that they got paid more for less work.

But also . . .

It's not fair that you've been given a second, third, or fiftieth chance. It's not fair that you've been given this day to live. It's not fair that you have clothes on your back and a roof over your head.

Why? Because someone else hasn't been given those things. Someone else wasn't given that chance. Attempting to determine the sliding scale of fair is not up to us. It's up to the Landowner himself. We can't understand or explain his system.

But we can learn to pay attention. We can open our eyes to the wonder around us. We can posture ourselves to receive the Good

News that is offered to us. We can ask for the grace that is freely available to us.

Those in despair, the poor and the needy, the brokenhearted, the captive, and the sinner—everyone who repents, who turns around and goes away from hatred toward healing—will one day be saved. Every area of failure in this life will be replaced by a Kingdom that will be established forever and ever. Where all the pain, all the suffering, and all the disappointment of your past will be wiped clean, and all the joy, all the excitement, and all the anticipation that is promised will be fulfilled.

This is the wonderful mystery of life with God. It's unexplainable. But it's not intended to be explained. It's intended to be pondered and wondered.

So give up trying to jockey for more than a day's wages. Forgive, receive forgiveness, and let go of your expectations about what is fair. Cultivate a spirit of humble curiosity. Revel in the fact that you've graciously inherited more than you ever needed or deserved.

Life is too short to live in the past of misplaced assumptions. Instead, accept the invitation. Let your past be redeemed. Let your assumptions be transformed. Let your life become marked by gratitude and appreciation for the forgiveness that God has given you.

5

FAILURE OBSESSED

WE HAVE A SECRET OBSESSION.

It's not something that shows up on the surface of our lives. You won't find it in an Instagram bio. But it's an obsession that permeates the very ethos of the human condition.

You know what it is? We love when people fail. That's right, I said it. We *love* when people fail. Don't believe me? Get on social media or the news site of your choice right now and start scrolling.[1] It's a continuum of one failure after another.

How this politician let us down . . . *again*. How this pastor had an affair. How this athlete missed the shot. How this fundamentalist got it wrong. How this business owner got caught stealing.

One of our great tragedies is how we equate "failure" with "finished." Because we don't want to be "finished," we hide our own failures while condemning the failures of others. The milieu of "cancel culture" epitomizes this way of thinking.

Now, before you cancel *me*, hear me out: I don't, in any way, want to diminish the hurt, pain, or brokenness caused by many individuals who have been justifiably called out. I am grateful for many of the (helpful) societal reforms that have come as a result of people in power being exposed. I believe in due process and that truth should win out.

However, we can be tempted to feed off of cynical conclusions rather than humble curiosity. Free expression and free speech have been polarized in a way that's made open debate and the tolerance of differences in opinion, outlook, or worldview almost unbearable.

In the wake of all this, many of us are simply checking out, numbing out, or bowing out from civil discourse that feeds genuine empathy, understanding, and connection. We're unwilling to admit our own failures and biases or engage with other viewpoints. Instead, we're content to listen to like-minded individuals who allow us to feel safe—even at the expense of our integrity.

The group to be wary of is what the journalist Conor Friedersdorf calls "the digital mob."[2] What we can fail to realize is just how often the "digital mob" *is* the group in power nowadays. And how often individuals have their integrity trampled without any chance to explain or hope for redemption. In an instant, livelihoods, careers, and legacies are dashed. Remember, the problem isn't that we make assumptions; it's that we assume too much. Our assumptions can carry us past the point of conviction into narrow-minded condemnation of others if we aren't careful. We are tempted to assume without taking the time to wisely discern what is true and what isn't—until we are the ones who fail.

The other day I found myself watching one of *those* Netflix documentaries. You know? The one about the famous person who had a tragic public meltdown and is now being exploited for millions of dollars to further crucify their character in front of the masses?

Is that interpretation a bit cynical? Perhaps. But when we take an honest look at our own hearts, we have to admit that there's a tendency to be both disgusted and invigorated by the failure of others. *What a creep. I would NEVER do something like that*, I found myself thinking as I watched the documentary. There's a part of human nature that feeds off failure. We deny, dismiss, and hide our own shortcomings while seeking content that highlights the failings of others. For many of us, especially in this cultural moment, failure seems final.

Why wouldn't it be? We often feel most threatened by what we most fear. A recent poll found that 31 percent of people fear failure. A larger percentage than the fear of spiders or being home alone.[3]

This fear of failure stunts our ability to discover a life of true purpose and meaning. The cultural pressures to perform and be perfect can feel almost overwhelming at times. It's a standard we're afraid to admit we can't live up to. And if we're unable to admit our own failures, what happens when someone fails us? Ohhh, the vengeance, the wrath, the anger, the vitriol we feel toward them. . . . It seethes within us.

Failure is *final*—for us, for them—so we say. Not, however, according to the Scriptures. What if Jesus invites us to a better way of life? A way of life where redemption, restoration, and renewal take place? Where failure is no longer equated with finality but with forgiveness? Where—on the other side of failure—is no longer rejection but redemption? Where we are free to ask for what we need most—grace?

Before you and me is the opportunity to be freed from our obsession with failure and instead, to find freedom in a God marked by forgiveness.

Jesus had a lot to say about lusting after the failure of others.

In John chapter 8, a group of religious leaders—called the Pharisees—"brought in a woman caught in adultery" to Jesus.[4] A few questions should arise: First, how was this woman caught engaging in such a private and intimate act? Also, where was the man caught in adultery? Foul play is surely to be suspected.

"They made her stand before the group and said to Jesus, 'Teacher, this woman was caught in the act of adultery.'"[5] This phrase, "made her stand," is a literal translation of the Greek verb *histémi*.[6] It implies force.

Now, we must keep in mind that Jesus is teaching publicly in the most iconic place in all of Jerusalem: the Temple. In other words, these Pharisees are not interested in justice; they're interested in creating a spectacle. This is a WWE match, mixed with an episode of Jerry Springer, being live streamed, all on steroids.

The intent is clear: ruthless humiliation. They're seeking to send a message.

The Pharisees tell Jesus that—according to the law of Moses—the woman deserves to be stoned (killed) for such an act. So now, in the middle of the public square, they want to know what Jesus has to say.[7] These are dangerous waters to be swimming in, and they know it.[8]

This is the moment.

Jesus begins cursing the woman and humiliating her even further . . . right? I mean, isn't that what she deserves? She's in the wrong. She's in sin. She's at fault. She's failed.

But that's not how Jesus responds. Instead of saying anything, Jesus *stoops*.

A stooped posture is one of humility. In this moment, Jesus could have towered over the woman in front of him. He could have driven the standing woman to her knees as he berated, chastised, and further shamed her. But he doesn't.

Jesus stoops.

To stoop is to posture yourself beneath another. This was a posture not just of submission but of solidarity. Jesus stooping was Jesus communicating, *I'm here. I see you. I love you.*

Jesus' posture is predictive of what is to come. Here, a woman stands naked and ashamed in front of a world ready to condemn her. A while later, Jesus stands naked on a cross, conquering shame, in front of a world ready to condemn him.

Jesus stooped from his throne of glory in heaven, from the right hand of God the Father, and he "being in very nature God, did not consider equality with God something to be used to his own advantage; rather, he made himself nothing by taking the very nature of a servant, being made in human likeness. And being found in appearance as a man, he humbled himself by becoming obedient to death—even death on a cross!"[9]

He bends down and starts writing on the ground. Now, most scholars agree that there can be no consensus on what exactly Jesus was writing, but there are a few interpretations that I find compelling:

A) He was writing a list of sins committed by each of the Jewish leaders present. This has a bit of angsty-rock Jesus to it that I vibe with. The justice side of me says, "Yeah, Jesus. Get 'em."

B) He was writing as a distraction to divert everyone's attention from the naked, ashamed woman present. The compassion side of me sees this option and thinks, *Of course Jesus would want to do everything possible to provide dignity and worth to an individual who had it all stripped away.*

C) He was doodling as a way of contemptuously disregarding the blatant hypocrisy. The thought of a sarcastic, presumptuous Jesus here makes me chuckle. This is like watching someone walk into the intellectual trap of a Jedi Master. *This isn't going to end well for you, my friend.*

But there's another alternative that I find most compelling: "Just as the Ten Commandments had been 'inscribed by the finger of God' (Exodus 31:18), whatever Jesus was writing was a subtle way of communicating to them that he himself was the divine author of the law. Writing on the dirt was also an allusion to the fact that the law had been given to mankind who had been created out of dust and were therefore vulnerable to weakness and sin."[10]

That.

I mean, here we have Jesus—the Savior of the world—unmistakably putting his finger into the dirt as if to make it painfully obvious: let's not forget who's in charge here.

It reminds me of the scene from the Chronicles of Narnia when Aslan interrupts the White Witch and says, "Do not cite the Deep Magic to me, Witch! I was there when it was written."[11]

Like, of course, how could the Pharisees ever pretend to know and understand the Law better than the One who wrote it in the first place?

My friends, Jesus didn't just stoop for this woman. He lowered himself for you and for me. Jesus *was* and *is* without sin. He *was* and *is* justified in throwing the first stone. But Jesus—in humility—took on the weight of our humiliation.

He did not dismiss the responsibility of repentance and righteousness. His final charge to this woman was "go now and leave your life of sin."[12]

And guess what? We don't hear from her again. So, can we infer that in this moment of grace, she listened? She did just that? She accepted the forgiveness offered to her and turned from her failure?

We are so quick to equate failure with being finished that we rarely afford others—or ourselves—a second chance. Grace, grace, grace has been given to us. It's free for the asking. Perhaps we should extend grace, grace, grace to others. *We are not the authors of the Law.* We were not there when it was written. But Jesus was.

Jesus' introspective question is one we should heed daily. *Which of you shall cast the first stone?* His question does not justify or diminish the wrong that has been done. It simply transfers the responsibility of punishment to the only one with the credibility to decide.

Do we trust and believe in the gospel we willingly proclaim? Because this gospel—this Good News—is for everyone. And for everyone, the statement is clear: "Therefore, there is now no condemnation for those who are in Christ Jesus."[13]

In an age of failure obsession, when we are tempted to vilify, crucify, and stone everyone in our wake, what if we became a people marked by reconciliation, hopeful restoration, and authentic accountability? What if we allowed our assumptions to be transformed and asked for forgiveness when we fail? What if we allowed the world to see the church of Jesus Christ as she was intended to be? A distinct counterculture. A light to the world. A city on a hill, which cannot be hidden.

It starts by dropping the first stone. Release your grip.

But the leaders don't catch the hint. They keep asking, keep prodding, and keep poking at Jesus. *Well Jesus, what do ya say?!*

Eventually, Jesus stands up and says, "'Let any one of you who is without sin be the first to throw a stone at her.' Again he stooped down and wrote on the ground."[14]

Mesmerizing.

Back to the ground he goes.

I am the Author. You are the page.

I am the Artisan. You are the clay.

I am the Creator. You are the creation.

The message begins to sink in. One by one—starting with the oldest—the Pharisees walk away.

I find it interesting that the oldest lead the way. Again, we're unsure of why, but my guess? The older ones had lived longer, which gave them more opportunities to sin. Perhaps their longer years ingrained more wisdom and humility to admit their faults and shortcomings. But I digress.

In this moment, only Jesus and the woman are left.

At this, he directly acknowledges the woman for the first time and asks where her accusers are and if anyone has condemned her. Her response? No one.[15]

This is the moment.

In this woman's time of greatest pain, she is set free. No longer is she bound by shame; instead, she is released into life to the full through the forgiveness of her sins. Her failure is revealed—and removed. She is chosen, redeemed, and accepted by her Lord and Savior. Out of this new identity, a new invitation is given. Go and sin no more.[16]

One of the truly fascinating aspects of Jesus' life is that the very people whose lives least aligned with his ethical teachings were the ones most drawn to him. His dinner company and close friends were made up of people out of alignment with his teaching (e.g., Jesus teaches that to even look at a woman lustfully is to commit adultery, yet here he is compassionately present with a woman caught in this sin).

This is what we—as followers of Jesus—are to model. We should be unapologetically aligned with every word of Jesus' teaching and committed to boldly upholding it. However, we must live and act in such a way that those out of alignment with our beliefs (such as those who don't follow Jesus) feel welcomed and accepted by us.[17]

This is the tension that we see Jesus beautifully navigate. And it is a similar tension that we are to uphold. Notice Jesus' final line to this woman, translated literally: "Go and from now [on] no more sin."[18] Jesus never agrees with or approves of the woman's choices. But he does accept and love her as a daughter of the Most High.

We can lovingly disapprove of another's actions without assassinating their character. It is the gracious home of love where failure isn't final that many prodigals feel compelled to return to.

Mercy, mercy, mercy, with justice in tow.

Corrie ten Boom was a Dutch watchmaker in the 1940s who—along with her family—joined the Dutch resistance against Nazi Germany, hiding Jewish refugees at the height of World War II. At one point, they were betrayed and turned over to the gestapo for their perceived criminal activity. Corrie and her elder sister, Betsie, were eventually sentenced to imprisonment at a concentration camp in Germany called Ravensbrück.

The horrid living conditions of Ravensbrück ended up contributing to Betsie's death. So much heartbreak and pain followed Corrie.

Eventually, Corrie was released and dedicated the rest of her life to traveling the world telling her and Betsie's story. In her memoir entitled *The Hiding Place*, Corrie shares about one of these speaking engagements where forgiveness was thrust to the forefront of her life. As she recalls later on, "It was in a church in Munich that I saw him, a balding heavyset man in a gray overcoat, a brown felt hat clutched between his hands."[19]

Corrie finishes preaching, and the man in the gray overcoat approaches her. In an instant, she is transported back to the place of her greatest hurt. And one of the men who caused all of it standing right in front of her. He audaciously approaches Corrie, sticks out his hand, and says, "A fine message, *fräulein*! How good it is to know that, as you say, all our sins are at the bottom of the sea!"[20]

In that moment, Corrie freezes. Everything she has just preached seems to be flying out the window. It is the first time that she has seen one of her captors face-to-face. The man continues, "You mentioned Ravensbrück in your talk. I was a guard in there. But since that time, I have become a Christian. I know that God has forgiven me for the cruel things I did there, but I would like to hear it from your lips as well. *Fräulein*"—again the hand came out—"will you forgive me?"[21]

Can you imagine? This was a man who had contributed to the death of Corrie's sister. A man who had repented, found Jesus, and was seeking a new life of reconciliation. A man asking forgiveness for what was seemingly unforgivable.

How was Corrie going to respond?

She writes it far better than I can describe:

> I stood there—I whose sins had every day to be forgiven—and could not. . . . "Jesus, help me!" I prayed silently. "I can lift my hand. I can do that much. You supply the feeling." And so woodenly, mechanically, I thrust my hand into the one stretched out to me. And as I did, an incredible thing took place. The current started in my shoulder, raced down my arm, sprang into our joined hands. And then this healing warmth seemed to flood my whole being, bringing tears to my eyes.
> "I forgive you, brother!" I cried. "With all my heart!"
> For a long moment we grasped each other's hands, the former guard and the former prisoner. I had never known God's love so intensely as I did then.[22]

At the essence of reconciliation is conviction. Both parties—those who were wronged and who have wronged—must be convicted to turn around and move toward one another rather than apart. This is not always possible nor wise. But when possible, it is a beautiful, backward picture of the gospel at work in our lives. Against all odds and against all logic, healing begins to take place when we ask for and offer forgiveness.

There is a great resonance to Corrie's story within all of us. Despite the atrocities done by this guard, Corrie's reaction to his request and subsequent reconciliation with this man should—in some way, shape, or form—elicit a feeling of deep relief. "This is how it's *supposed* to be." Because it is. Reconciliation and restoration are the aim of God himself. A new heaven and a new earth are coming. The old will pass away and the new will come. Forgiveness will be extended, and reconciliation will cement itself forevermore. But until that day arrives, we are tasked with the heavenly work on earth now.

Hearing a story like the guard approaching Corrie for forgiveness or Jesus offering grace to the woman caught in adultery can be intensely liberating if we are the one who has messed up and are seeking forgiveness.

But what about if we're the wronged party in this situation? What if we are the ones with every right to demand justice and accountability? The religious leaders in John 8 don't seem to be directly connected to this woman. Could they have been to the man? Perhaps. Either way, a plain reading of the text shows that their intent was to humiliate her not hold her accountable.

True justice would've required two things:

1. A witness (there seems to be none because in Jewish law, the witness was the one to cast the first stone)

2. The accused (only the woman is present, not the man, implying that this was a hit job on an individual)

Jesus is not giving this woman a free pass, though. He doesn't say, "Don't execute her." He simply puts the situation into perspective. What's your real motive? What are your assumptions? Are you seeking what is right, or are you seeking revenge?

What about us? I see cancel culture all over here, picking up our stones, ready to lob via texting thumbs and Twitter (X) timelines. *See, I told you so! Boom goes the dynamite! They had it coming.*

Honestly, these are G-rated synopses of some vulgar comments that users have posted on click-bait articles regarding people's public failure.

We can't wait to cast the first stone. We don't want to shake the other person's hand.

But have we ever stopped to consider Jesus' response? Again, "Let any one of you who is without sin be the first to throw a stone at her."[23]

Jesus is calling to mind the weight of the sin that has been committed in this situation. A woman has been caught in adultery. That's objectively bad. No one is arguing against that.

How about a group of religious leaders orchestrating a plot to humiliatingly murder this woman under the guise of holiness but really with a greater agenda toward trapping Jesus? That's reprehensible—according to Jesus.

This story has echoes of Jesus' parable in Matthew 7. Jesus says in his Sermon on the Mount that those who judge will be judged. In fact, to the same degree we judge others, we will be judged.[24]

Jesus then offers a helpful word picture. He says, "Why do you look at the speck of sawdust in your brother's eye and pay no attention to the plank in your own eye? How can you say to your brother, 'Let me take the speck out of your eye,' when all the time there is a plank in your own eye? You hypocrite, first take the plank out of your own eye, and then you will see clearly to remove the speck from your brother's eye."[25] Before pointing out others' failures, remember your own need to ask for forgiveness.

Now, you might roll your eyes and say, "That's not *fair*! Where is the justice?! Where are the consequences? Where is the hurt, the pain, and the embarrassment they *deserve*?"

Perhaps your sentiments are worse. Maybe in a fit of rage you are ready to fling your stone as hard as you possibly can. But the guard, the woman caught in adultery, the person you are holding bitterness toward has already been released. Jesus has declared to them, "Go now and leave your life of sin." Forgiveness has been freely offered to them just as it has been offered to you.

For you, though, maybe the situation has morphed. It's no longer about justice but about judgment. And now? Well now, it's just you and Jesus and your stone. What are you going to do? You might be ready to throw a stone at the one you really believe deserves it. Jesus himself.

Here's how John 8 closes: "'Very truly I tell you,' Jesus answered, 'before Abraham was born, I am!' At this, they picked up stones to stone him, but Jesus hid himself, slipping away from the temple grounds."[26]

Are you starting to sense the complexity and difficulty of Jesus' instruction to forgive and ask for forgiveness? Know that there is so much sympathy from me. This is hard. I get it wrong all the time. But if I can gently offer this idea to you, I really think Jesus is less concerned about the practice of forgiveness itself and more concerned with the posture of your heart.

Here's what I mean. We can't walk away from this thinking, *Well, I can just do whatever I want because God is going to forgive me anyway* or *What's the point of caring when anyone does something wrong, they're just going to be pardoned regardless?* We're missing the point if that's our takeaway. Jesus never says, "Don't uphold justice." There is a time and a place to rebuke those who are in sin. Jesus preaches about and models the practice countless times throughout the New Testament.[27] The religious leaders' error is not in practice but posture.

When we rebuke, what is our motive?

Is it conviction or condemnation? Is it gracious love or unrighteous anger? Is it restoration or retribution? Are we willing to accept the offered hand of our enemy?

When we ask for forgiveness, have we truly taken responsibility for our actions? Or are we only looking to get rid of our guilt? Have we questioned our assumptions and confessed our failures? Are we ready to receive grace?

Jesus' posture is one of release, not resentment. It's one of invitation, not intimidation. He doesn't try to escalate the situation and stoke the fire. He is a peacemaker. He is firm but not fierce. He holds all the feelings of this moment—the woman's shame and the leaders' scorn—in perfect tension.

So, my friend, are you thriving off of the failure around you? Are you willing to cast the first stone? If so, somehow, someway, the only person it's going to hurt in the end is you.

Perhaps it's time to unsubscribe from the tabloids. Maybe you need to unfollow or mute a few social media accounts. Perhaps you need to give yourself a break from the online debates you so frequently engage in. Maybe you need to detox from the high you feel as you focus on the failure of others. Maybe you need to ask for forgiveness.

Whatever fix you're getting from propping yourself up on people's failures is only going to widen the chasm within your soul. That gap cannot be filled with the failure of others. Their mistakes can't erase your own. The emptiness can only be filled by the forgiveness that Jesus offers to you and me—if we only ask.

6

COME OUT OF HIDING

I WAS IN THE FOURTH GRADE the first time that I was exposed to pornography.

I had been invited over to my neighbor, Tyler's, house to spend the night. Tyler had one of those old Macs with the blue plastic back on it. You remember those? His house was one of my favorite places to be. At Tyler's house, there were no rules. We could stay up as late as we wanted, watch whatever we wanted, play whatever we wanted, and eat whatever we wanted. It was the dream life for a ten-year-old.

Until the day pornography entered the picture.

"Dude, you have to come see this."

What could he possibly be so excited about?

As I entered his room, there—around the corner—sat his blue plastic Mac with the screen lit up. My stomach dropped, and my heart raced.

"I don't think we're supposed to be looking at this."

For seven years, that initial exploration in Tyler's room remained dormant and stuffed in the back of my mind. I didn't tell anyone about it, and I didn't think any more of it.

Until I turned seventeen. And a long-term girlfriend and I broke up. I experienced real feelings of rejection, loneliness, and despair for the first time.

It was in that emotional and vulnerable state that Tyler's room once again began to beckon. A simple google search devolved into a seven-year, full-fledged pornography addiction. An addiction that I hid, dismissed, and then justified. At first, I was a young, single teen whose hormones—I told myself—gave me permission to explore. Before finally I ended up a young, married husband whose exploits began causing severe, near-irreversible damage to a new and fragile marriage.

This was the third time that I had to work up the courage to confess something that I was hiding to Rylei over the course of our—at that time—six-year relationship.

The first instance occurred in the front seat of her car one random Friday night after a date. We were starting to have serious conversations about marriage, and Rylei—out of nowhere—said, "I have a strong sense that you've kept something from me."

I was stuck. There was nowhere to run or hide. Our car was parked, and I couldn't think of a way to get out of there fast enough. So, I sheepishly replied, "You're right. There is." And as I confessed what I had hidden from her, she told me that she wasn't upset about what I had done, she was upset that I didn't feel safe enough to trust her.

To be honest, I didn't trust her because I didn't believe her. I didn't believe that if I told her about what I was hiding, she'd want to stay with me. I didn't think that she would forgive or accept me.

A few years later, Rylei and I were married and living on our own in the middle of nowhere, Illinois. It was a quaint, quiet town, but we were twenty-one and had no idea how to do life—on our own, much less together. Marriage had not solved my pornography addiction—what I eventually found out, through counseling, was a coping mechanism for all the feelings of rejection, failure, and insecurity that I had accrued over time.

So, a week after our first Valentine's Day as a married couple, Rylei and I were sitting in our barely-furnished living room attempting to endure the Midwest blizzard outside when she again—out of nowhere—asked, "Are you hiding something from me?" The doors were locked, and our one car was in the garage. There was no escape.

"Uhh . . . uh . . . I uh . . ."

She already knew.

She decided to take a chance on the weather and left the house for a few hours to process, leaving me in the wake of a massive cloud that I was beginning to form around our marriage.

Another few years passed. We had moved into our first home, and after almost a year of sobriety, the stress of moving, a massive transition at my workplace, and relational tension in my own life began to push me over the abyss back toward pornography as an escape.

This time around, when Rylei asked, I skirted and skated and dodged her questions like I was in *The Matrix*. Eventually, the truth came out.

Rylei left. Three strikes.

That's where I found myself the evening that I called Nick on our front porch, my body trembling. "Nick, it's Micah."

"What's up, man?"

"I need to talk to you and Jamie."

He knew it was serious.

From there, I confessed to my mentor and his wife that I had been hiding a pornography addiction for the better part of a year. Worse still, Nick was a man I deeply respected who had checked in on me every single month and had specifically asked if I was looking at anything I wasn't supposed to.

I'd lied every time.

As I shared the truth, I couldn't stop crying. I was sorry that I had lied. I was sorry that I had sinned. I was angry that I couldn't shake the addiction. I was embarrassed. I was ashamed. I was at my end. But more than anything, I was crushed at how deeply I had hurt Rylei.

I'll never forget what Jamie, Nick's wife, said to me that night on our phone call. She was righteously angry at me, heartbroken for Rylei, but calm and collected in her response. Her words became the starting line of our forgiveness journey. "Micah, Rylei is deservedly angry and hurt. You need to let her be. Give her space. But when the time comes and she chooses to forgive you, believe her. And live out of that forgiveness as your heavenly Father forgives you."

Recently, I was reading through the Old Testament. In 1 Kings, one line in particular began popping up repeatedly. It made my heart race with a confusing mix of emotions—anger and indignation but also delight and surprise.

Here's one of the first times this line appears: "Solomon answered, 'You have shown great kindness to your servant, my father David, because he was faithful to you and righteous and upright in heart. You have continued this great kindness to him and have given him a son to sit on his throne this very day.'"[1]

Perhaps you're not familiar with David's story and are unsure why I reacted with such conflicting emotions.

What's the big deal? Sounds like this David guy was a good dude. Sounds like his reign went well. It sounds like Solomon could use a few pointers from his father, David!

Here's why I found myself in a space of such frustration: David wasn't faithful. David wasn't full of integrity. David didn't live righteously. If you're unfamiliar with the character arc of David's life, it's vastly different from what 1 Kings seems to eulogize.

From the time of his youth, David was set apart. A prophet named Samuel comes in search of the next King of Israel. David shows up, and God says, "Rise and anoint him; this is the one."[2]

After years in obscurity and on the run from King Saul, David eventually rises through the ranks and claims the throne that Samuel anointed him to all those years earlier. And for a time, David reigns righteously over Israel.

But then, a single moment changes the narrative of David's life. From his palace roof he sees a woman named Bathsheba bathing. He requests for her to come to the palace, learns that she's married to one of his soldiers, disregards that fact, sleeps with her, and impregnates her.[3]

In fear of being found out, David then has Bathsheba's husband, Uriah, brought home. David wines and dines Uriah multiple times, hoping that he'll go home to his wife so the whole event will be covered up (remember, there's no DNA testing to prove what really occurred).[4] But David's plan doesn't work, so he sends Uriah to the front lines of the war being fought for Israel—a war being fought, in some part, for King David himself—and he instructs the general of his army, Joab, to command everyone to abandon Uriah there to die, which they do.

David then takes Bathsheba—Uriah's wife—as his own.[5]

How are we feeling now about David's righteousness, faithfulness, and integrity?

The consequences of David's sin are enormous. Eventually, his life and reign begins to crash and burn all around him. It's a tragic story of a good man and family giving in to a depth of sin and depravity previously incomprehensible.

So for David to be cast in a light of faithfulness, righteousness, and uprightness seems not only unfair but untrue. These descriptors enraged me at first. Perhaps these descriptors enrage you too.

As you can recall, infidelity is a sin that has greatly affected my family for generations. As I read David's story, I read with a mix of fear and anger at the origin story that I was born into. I wondered if, like David, I was destined to simply repeat the sins of my father's (and his father before him) past.

But David's story doesn't end there. At some point, something flipped in him. The sins of his past began affecting his present.

Throughout time, God has used prophets as conduits to communicate particular messages of (often hard) truth. In David's case, God used the prophet Nathan to expose David for the sinner he was and the hypocrite he had become.

Nathan tells David a story about two men in a town—one who was rich and one who was poor.[6] The rich man had everything he could ever need, but the poor man only had one little lamb to survive on.

A guest stopped at the rich man's house for a meal. Rather than sacrificing one of his own—many—animals for a meal, the rich man went and took the poor man's cherished lamb. David was outraged.

"WHO COULD DO THIS?"

"WHAT A &#^@*!"

"WHY I OUGHTA . . ."

It's the sins of our past that most often trigger us in our present.

Nathan had David right where he wanted him as he emphatically declared, "David, YOU. ARE. THAT. MAN." In this moment, something broke in David. Finally, the weight of his sinful choices had caught up to him.

As I read this passage with conflicting emotions, I felt the Holy Spirit whisper, *What about you? You're angry at David, but what about you? You're bitter about the generational sin in your family, but you attempt to use the past as an excuse and justification for your unfaithful present. What about you?*

My anger toward David isn't justified unless I'm willing to show the same anger toward myself. The condemnation I express toward my forefathers is irrelevant unless I'm willing to condemn myself to the same fate.

I had no reason to be incensed, judgmental, or dismissive toward David—the adulterer. I have committed adultery in my heart more times than I can count.

I could not shame, blame, or gripe about David coveting another man's wife. I was addicted to doing the same through a screen for *years*.

The honest truth is, *you* are that man. And so am I.

There may be those of you reading this who are looking for any excuse—as a follower of Jesus—*not* to forgive. I hate to spoil it for you, but you won't find one. "For all have sinned and fall short of the glory of God, and all are justified freely by his grace through the redemption that came by Christ Jesus."[7]

But there are others of you who are full of so much guilt and shame for whatever it is you've done that it's taking everything in you right now to turn the page. Deep down, you're ashamed. You're wondering how in the world God—or anyone, for that matter—could ever forgive you. You're pleading for a second, third, or fiftieth chance, hoping that it will be given but expecting the rejection you've felt your entire life.

It's those of you looking for forgiveness that I want to speak to in the remainder of this chapter. To you and me, forgiveness is available. But it's a process. Here's how that process works.

Remorse

In order to authentically receive forgiveness, you must be genuinely sorry for what you've done or who you've hurt. Forgiveness may be extended to you despite an absence of remorse, but you can't receive it unless you are genuinely sorry for what you've done.

We must feel the magnitude and weight of our sin. This is a good thing. God does not bring us face-to-face with our sin to shame or condemn us. Rather, he shows us our sin to reveal how powerless and not in control we are. How desperately we need his grace.

The first time I publicly confessed my pornography addiction was to my dad the day before my twentieth birthday. I had been struggling in secret for nearly three years. After the conversation with my dad, I told Rylei, "I don't want to take this into my twenties."

Rylei and I had only been dating for about six months when all of this came out for the first time. My confession was met by Rylei and my father with an expected sorrow but appreciation. "Thank you for your honesty" and "I'm proud of you" were some of their sentiments.

The problem was, I believed that confession would be a magic switch. Like I could turn off three years of consistent pornography intake *like that.* My confession came from a desire to be *better*, not because I had become *broken*. I didn't feel the consequences or weight of my sinful choices . . . yet.

But almost three years into marriage, Rylei met my next confession with an ultimatum. "Micah, you choose. Pornography or our marriage. Because I refuse to continue down this road."

Rylei was my Nathan.

YOU. ARE. THAT. MAN. The weight of my sin had finally sunk in.

Psalm 51 offers us insight into the moment where David finally feels the weight of his sin. It begins like this:

> Have mercy on me, O God,
>   according to your unfailing love;
> according to your great compassion
>   blot out my transgressions.
> Wash away all my iniquity
>   and cleanse me from my sin.[8]

These are the words I found myself praying late into the night. Rylei had kicked me out of the bedroom, and I found myself in our bonus room—what had essentially become a storage room until it would hopefully become a nursery. In the corner was an old chair Rylei was trying to sell. I fell to my knees and wept, the full moon shining through the curtainless window into the dark room.

As I prayed Psalm 51, I felt the full weight of my sins and transgressions. I sensed the pain and hurt that I had caused. And I knew that a change needed to be made. The stakes were too high, and I did not want to lose the person who I most loved.

Recourse

If you feel true remorse, then in order to receive forgiveness, you must commit to recourse. You must choose a new way of life. In the Scriptures, this is referred to as repentance.

In Greek, to repent is the word *metanoeō*, and it means to turn around or to go another direction.[9] To repent—to turn around—is actionable.

I remember sitting in intensive counseling feeling incensed and utterly disrespected by our marriage counselor. Her instructions to Rylei were plain and simple: "If Micah relapses in the next thirty days, you kick him out of the bedroom for thirty days."

Thirty . . . days?! I immediately became internally defensive. *Who does she think she is? This is ridiculous. Why is she being so unfair?*

In a moment when I had hurt Rylei, I was still trying to play the victim. This is exactly what our marriage counselor was attempting to expose. The true essence of a broken and contrite heart is one that is not defensive because it has nothing to prove, nothing to lose, and nothing to hide.[10] For whatever reason, I felt that I had everything to prove and everything to lose. I had become incredibly skilled at hiding.

In addition to accepting the thirty-day guideline, I had to begin attending an addiction recovery group for thirteen straight weeks every Monday night from 7-9 p.m. I was thoroughly embarrassed and ashamed to have to admit my failures and weaknesses to others. We began our first session similar to how Alcoholics Anonymous does. I opened up with "Hi, my name is Micah, and I'm addicted to pornography."

Humiliating. But necessary. My pride needed to be stomped out. My posture needed to become defenseless. I had sinned, and I needed to change my ways. I wouldn't change without knowing that continuing down my current trajectory would lead to losing everything I most cared about. I needed to feel the high stakes. Consequences became a gracious gift in understanding that.

The true evidence of recourse—of change—comes in our response.

On the first night of recovery group, my counselor asked me, "Micah, what are you willing to do to restore trust in your marriage?" I quietly replied, "Whatever it takes." I had arrived at a point where I had no other recourse than to press into Jesus.

Remorse and recourse are found in a "whatever it takes" mindset.

When we're willing to pursue reconciliation—no matter the cost—as the offender in a situation, we discover hope.

Recommit

The real turning point in my journey came a week after the night that I confessed my pornography addiction to Rylei almost three years into our marriage.

We were out to dinner with six of our closest friends. It was the beginning of spring and just warm enough to sit outside. At this quaint little barbecue joint, we went around the table sharing updates about life—including marriage. I knew that I had a choice: I could spin the last week of our lives in a way that didn't make me out to be a total embarrassment, probably incurring more of Rylei's anger later but saving my public dignity.[11] Or I could come clean. *Create in me a pure heart, O God*, I remembered. Psalm 51 was everywhere in my mind.

So that night, I shared everything again—this time with six others around the table. Looking into my wife's eyes as I confessed my addiction was painful. But equally as painful was looking into the eyes of the three *other* women around the table who represented the very people that I had routinely objectified and dehumanized.

Here I was, afraid and so, so vulnerable. However, in that confession, I was shocked to be received into a community that was not without consequences and correction but was without judgment and shame. It was that group of friends who helped me believe that forgiveness and restoration were possible.

Community is central to the forgiveness journey.

Whatever it is that you have repented of, let others in. Tell them about what you are asking God to change. Let them hold you accountable to depend on the Holy Spirit for that transformation to take place.

To be clear, this is hard. It takes work. And it's often painfully inconvenient or inefficient. I can't recall the number of times my first year of recovery that Rylei was out of town and I had to meet a friend in a public space to unlock my phone and perform a basic function because of all the restrictions that were on it. But the freedom I experienced regarding having nothing to prove, nothing to lose, and nothing to hide was worth it.

There is nothing you can do to earn God or anyone else's forgiveness. But you can work to build back credibility. So, turn around. Go a different way. Daily recommit to living in the light as God restores your present and redeems the darkness in your past.

Restore

When we're on the receiving end of forgiveness, the only form of currency we have to build back trust and credibility is time.

When someone chooses to forgive you, the debt is wiped clean. There should be no barrier of bitterness or resentment. But wise boundaries and restorative measures should be put into place. Why? Because something has been broken. When a vase shatters, it can't be scooped up whole. If it is to be restored, it must be put back together one piece at a time.

Forgiveness is instant. Trust and healing take time.

This, again, is good. In our instantaneous world, we hate to wait. But while giving and receiving forgiveness is an instantaneous action, the process of healing, repair, and reconciliation is just that . . . a process.

We can express remorse, choose a different way, and recommit to that new way over the long haul, showing that our transformation is genuine and real.

So, find moments—daily—to restore credibility and trust with those you've wounded. To this day, if I get a pornographic spam email or accidentally see something that is tempting, I make it a point to tell Rylei, even if it doesn't show up on my accountability software. Why? I want to live from the new way of life that I chose all those years ago. A posture of "nothing to prove, nothing to lose, nothing to hide." Out of the dark and into the light.

(Be) Renewed

No matter whether the person you've hurt chooses to forgive you, we all must get to a place where we understand that, as sons and daughters of God, we are *forgiven*.

Forgiveness's power is not dependent on *feeling* forgiven. When we seek God, we find forgiveness.[12] In Christ, we are forgiven.

The longer we live in unbelief, the more we miss out on the beautiful gift of grace that God offers us. We don't have to wallow in sin or make excuses for it. Instead, we declare—by the power and blood of the slain Lamb—that we are forgiven, redeemed, restored, and renewed.

Here's David in Psalm 103:

> He does not deal with us according to our sins,
> > nor repay us according to our iniquities.
> For as high as the heavens are above the earth,
> > so great is his steadfast love toward those who fear him.[13]

Could it be that David was able to internalize this message? Despite his sin, despite his shortcomings, might he be counted as righteous, upright, pure, and of integrity because he realized not who he was but who God is?

Here's the best part . . . for David, for you, and for me, the slate is wiped clean. All of us who belong to Christ Jesus, who have sworn our allegiance to him, who are his apprentices—no matter our past, our mistakes, our hurt or bitterness, our regrets—are free recipients of *grace*. As a son or daughter of God, mercy is accessible to you.

Our beautifully broken lives become examples of what it looks like to faithfully follow Jesus in the way of forgiveness—both given and received.

Your life matters. No matter what you've done or how you've messed up, you matter to God. And he has placed a call on your life.

God wants to use you, every part of you—your flaws, failures, fears, doubts, strengths, gifts, talents, and abilities—to change this world as we know it. To help bring heaven on earth.

Rylei left that night, and I assumed that I had struck out. The umpire of my past was cruelly taunting me.

But, over time, as I expressed remorse, set a new course, recommitted to Jesus' way of integrity and fidelity, and embraced the process of restoration, I discovered that the game wasn't over for me. It wasn't over for David. And it doesn't have to be over for you.

If you find yourself in need of forgiveness, know that we serve a God who says, **three strikes, you're . . . forgiven.**

7

PUT IT TO USE

I WAS ANGRY. NO, I WAS HURT. Actually, I was feeling let down.

All these emotions and more spilled out toward my friend, Matt, on a dark Friday morning in November.

For context, Matt and I are best friends. He's a part of what we call our "covenant community." A group of six (three couples) that we've pledged to do life with.

The rub? Covenanting yourself to someone means loving them—for better or worse.

When you're in tune, when the vibes are good, and when the conversation is flowing, covenant community is a gift. But when disagreements arise, people are absent, or life happens, well . . . it becomes less of an ideal and more of an intentional decision.

The prior few months had been a whirlwind for both Matt and me. I was in the throes of planting a church and releasing a book. Matt was releasing new music, managing some intense family challenges, moving into a new house (a mile down the road from us), and attempting to provide for his family in a myriad of ways.[1] The environment was ripe for stress, and distance became our preferred method of coping.

Our hangouts felt dry and empty. In fact, for the first time in our relationship, I dreaded being together. When we were, little things would annoy me. My temper was quick, and my patience was thin.

A root of bitterness was beginning to grow in my soul. And I made it known through my passive-aggressive actions and attitude. Rather than saying anything about the situation, I allowed all of this hurt to fester . . . for months.

Matt, Jake, and I—as part of our community rule of life—typically get together for breakfast once a month for an intentional check-in on one another. Finally, after a brief hiatus, we reconvened.

The scene was awkward at first. We had some short small talk in the mostly empty coffee shop before I decided I'd had enough of being two-faced.

"Matt, I have something I need to talk to you about. I need to share with you some resentment I've been holding on to for the last few months toward you and Kass."

Matt's face surprisingly didn't scream, "I can't wait for you to tell me this." (Once again, sarcasm, folks. Smile. It'll help ease the tension.)

Honestly, the more I talked, the more intense the conversation got.

I began to unload all my (what I perceived to be justified) hurt onto Matt. He took most of it in stride and humbly heard my critiques. However, he pushed back in a few key areas where he sensed bitterness rather than a caring rebuke.

I took his pushback as defensiveness, and the gloves came off (with both of us talking louder than was probably appropriate for the setting) right as one of our church's board members entered the coffee shop.

"Hey, fellas."

"Hey, David," I said dismissively. David got the hint and kept moving toward the coffee line.

David, who oversees the health of my soul and interior world, was watching me rip into not just my best friend but a congregant at our church—the church that David oversees.

Suddenly, ego and public perception took center stage. I was not in a good place. I started to pray that Matt would get the hint and tone down the volume a bit to save me the embarrassment of arguing in front of a board member who could hear our entire conversation. He didn't. He shouldn't.

"I understand where you're coming from, but some of these expectations were plainly unrealistic for where Kass and I found ourselves in this present moment," Matt said.

I was fuming at this point.

Why can't you just shut up and say you're wrong?

Why won't you tell me I'm right?

Why won't you listen?

You're such a ____, you know that?

I didn't say any of these things, of course, but I was thinking them. Matt probably was too. Jake sat there like the peaceful third party he was, as we sparred across the table. But you know what? Matt was right.

In that moment, I knew he was right. But all the pride, ego, and selfishness that I felt had been exposed continued to pressurize, and more than anything, I wanted to engage in fight or flight.

It's true. I—in all my sinfulness—wanted to either punch my best friend in the face or bolt for the door never to be seen again.

Perhaps you've found yourself in a similar place during conflict? There's something about conflict that brings the worst parts of us to the surface. The anger, resentment, passivity, envy, the ____ (you fill in the blank). It eats at us, fighting tooth and nail to keep us from the only exercise that will relieve the tension: forgiveness.

Forgiveness was the last thing that I wanted to ask Matt for at the time. But it was also the thing I most wanted.

This dichotomy expresses the tension many of us often feel. We want what we're unwilling to give. And the only way to get what we desperately need—according to Jesus—is to offer what's desperately needed.

―――

Essentially, to forgive means

1. to pardon;

2. to excuse someone from having to pay a debt they owe you.[2]

This last example is what we see laid out all throughout Scripture.

Here's Jesus in Matthew 6: "Forgive us our debts, as we also have forgiven our debtors."[3] The word "forgive" is the Greek word *aphiēmi*, which means to release or surrender a debt.[4]

Jesus shares another, more in-depth example of this definition of forgiveness in Matthew 18. The story goes: there was a servant who owed the king ten thousand bags of gold.[5] The Bible calls these *talents*. It's a ridiculous amount of money. Most commentators estimate this sum to be anywhere between twelve million and one billion US dollars.[6] Again, it's a rough estimate. But the point? It's a huge amount of debt. A debt so large that the average person could not pay it back over a lifetime.

The king, with no other way to recover his money, summons the servant with his family and all that he owns to be sold as collateral for the sum he'd lost. The servant begs for mercy and pleads with the king to reconsider.[7]

Then something miraculous happens. The king "took pity on him, canceled the debt and let him go."[8]

That phrase—"canceled the debt"—is, you guessed it, *aphiēmi*. This is a wild, lavish show of grace on the part of the king. But the feel-good story doesn't last long.

Upon leaving, the servant goes and finds another servant who owes him one hundred silver coins. The Scriptures call these *denarii*, and the sum (roughly one hundred days' worth of wages) is much less valuable than the debt the servant originally owed the king.[9] This fellow servant pleads with the servant in the same way the servant pleaded with the king to have mercy on him. But instead, the servant throws him into prison until he can repay the debt.[10]

Others see this take place and—sensing the extreme injustice of it all—take their disapproval to the king. The king then summons the servant back to him and declares, "'You wicked servant, I canceled all that debt of yours because you begged me to. Shouldn't you have had mercy on your fellow servant just as I had on you?' In anger his master handed him over to the jailers to be tortured, until he should pay back all he owed."[11]

Jesus finishes this teaching by stating, "This is how my heavenly Father will treat each of you unless you forgive your brother or sister from your heart."[12] Here's a Jesus one-liner for you to summarize all of this: "Blessed are the merciful, for they will be shown mercy."[13]

There seems to be a great emphasis placed on forgiveness by this Rabbi from Nazareth.

In case the point isn't clear: Forgive and you will be forgiven. Don't forgive and you won't be forgiven. Sounds straightforward, but we're all aware of how difficult this is, right? Forgiving is

Put It to Use

counterintuitive to everything we feel as human beings, and it's certainly countercultural to the world we live in today.

What most of our society fails to realize is that, in withholding what we are to give, we miss out on receiving the very thing we need. And it comes at a cost either way.

To forgive costs us greatly. However, to *not* forgive might end up costing us more. Do you know anyone with a deep-seated bitterness and resentment who has lived as a person marked by joy, peace, kindness, and love? I don't.

Forgiveness flies in the face of all things rational, coherent, and equal. It's fundamentally unequal, irrational, and incoherent. It's lavish. It's merciful. It's abundant. It's necessary in experiencing what Jesus calls life and life to the full. We must put forgiveness into practice. Easier said than done.

So where might we begin? How can we be shaped and formed into a person who is even able—much less desires—to forgive over and over and over again?

I believe we can embrace forgiveness through a practice that historically has been known as confession. Confession—at its best—is an acknowledgment of our sin before God and before other brothers and sisters in Christ, an invitation to receive forgiveness, and a commitment to live differently henceforth. When we look at Jesus' life and the Scriptures as a whole, confession is a central theme.

For instance, take the book of Psalms—specifically, Psalms 6, 32, 38, 51, 102, 130, and 143. These are known as the penitential Psalms or the Psalms of confession.

All throughout Jesus' ministry, he encountered people who desired healing. In an effort to receive healing, they *confessed* their brokenness. Look at the language used in Matthew 15: "Lord, son of

David, have mercy on me."[14] Or in Luke 17: "Jesus, Master, have pity on us!"[15] Or in Matthew 20: "Lord, Son of David, have mercy on us!"[16]

I could keep going, but you get the idea. In each of these instances, people came before Jesus broken and humble, asking him to do what only he can do—overcome their deficiencies and make them whole.

What if we were to see our spiritual deficiencies and approach Jesus with the same mindset as these people did? What if this sort of posture—a broken and contrite heart, as David calls it—is the only posture where true forgiveness can take root?[17]

Earlier in Luke 17, Jesus says, "Pay attention to yourselves! If your brother sins, rebuke him, and if he repents, forgive him."[18] There is a clear imperative here. If someone sins against you, tell them. Tell them why what they did was wrong and hurtful. But if they are sorry, forgive them. It is unloving to both not call out the sin and not forgive the sin. Love is the aim. And it starts with a sober examination of who? "Yourselves." Humility is required if we are to engage in this practice faithfully.

In Matthew 5, Jesus says, "So if you are offering your gift at the altar and there remember that your brother has something against you, leave your gift there before the altar and go. First be reconciled to your brother, and then come and offer your gift."[19] Once again, we see Jesus' intentional focus on the heart over outward actions. Offering praise and worship to Jesus with a heart full of anger and bitterness is white noise. Instead, we are to bring our broken and contrite heart to Jesus and allow him to transform us from the inside out. To release the prisoner we're holding captive. And to forgive—to seek reconciliation.

Throughout the New Testament, we see writers such as Peter, John, and James share similar sentiments.[20] The concepts of confession and forgiveness are clearly intertwined throughout the entirety of Scripture. And confession is a practice I think many of us stand to gain from.

The problem is—as already noted—we live in a cancel culture not a confessional culture.

For so long, I thought that as a Christian, then a leader, and eventually a pastor, I couldn't confess my sins and brokenness because it would disqualify me. I figured that if I let God in on my shortcomings (even though he already knew them), he would stop using me. I thought that if I let other people in my life in on the darkness of my heart and soul, they'd reject me.

I wonder how many of us are bound by the same lies I believed. I wonder if you, dear reader, can resonate. If we are ever going to become people of reconciliation and restoration, then we must create space for people to be their authentic selves. And you know what that requires? Forgiveness. Why?

Because other people will fail you. They will make mistakes. They will fall short. They will mess up. And so will you.

Confession is offered to us as a conduit to break free of the shame that sin holds over us.

I'm not sure what comes to mind when you hear the word *confession*. For me, it's Macaulay Culkin in *Home Alone* going to the church to be absolved from his sins.

Maybe for you, confession feels uncomfortable or unfamiliar. Perhaps it's a neutral word—something you know Catholics do but have not had much, if any, experience with. Or maybe it's a term you've embraced as part of your spiritual practice.

Over time, I've come to see the idea of the Catholic confessional booth as beautiful. What the booth does is create a space where people feel safe for their true selves to be seen. However, where the confessional booth falls short is in its ability to hold someone accountable to consequences.

Consequences are the result of our sinful actions. And consequences are one means by which we are sanctified—or made pure. At their best, consequences remind us of what is lost when we do not live up to a particular standard of character. Consequences motivate us to actively change and to pray to Jesus for transformation.

Know that when I say confession, I do not mean a complete absolving of hurt. Rather, I believe that we must create a space—similar to a confessional booth—where others can be fully known and loved despite their shortcomings and failures. A space where people will not fear being ostracized, rejected, or abandoned. From there, it is God who does the healing.

My friends, if we are to recover our ability to forgive and be forgiven, confession is the way forward. The three most healing words, "I forgive you," have to become a part of our vocabulary. And that can only be done through the regular practice of confession.

So, a few best practices:

1. I'D SUGGEST ENTERING INTO CONFESSION WITH SOMEONE YOU KNOW IS TRUSTWORTHY.

This is, quite frankly, where many of us get stumped. You might not have anyone trustworthy in your life. Only 32 percent of Americans thirty and under say that they have five or more close friends. Forty-nine percent of adults sixty-five and older say the same.[21] We are trending the wrong direction in terms of being known and loved.

We are desiring something we can neither give nor receive because forgiveness divorced from relationship is stagnant. Martin Luther King Jr. said, "Forgiveness means reconciliation, a coming together again."[22] There is a relational element to forgiveness that heals us. And without confession, we risk allowing God's forgiveness to be known in our head but not experienced in our heart. We fail to allow Jesus to turn wounds into scars.

We must learn to normalize confession in the context of relationship. Because in this safe space, forgiveness doesn't just absolve. People are held accountable, and eventually, changed and healed.

Matt, Jake, and I have lived in covenant community together now for years. I consider them to be my closest friends. Our ability to confess our frustrations and fears, sorrows and secrets, have come from a deep well of relational equity. I also have a group of pastors I belong to called "The Brotherhood." Eight of us who—like me, Matt, and Jake—abide by a communal rule of life together, which includes biweekly confession. If you, too, want to experience healing and transformation, I encourage you to find community.

So, begin processing who that safe individual might be for you. If you don't have someone, what is one step this week you could take to kindle such a friendship? You don't need to reach out to someone for coffee and dump all your darkest secrets onto them immediately. Instead, reach out to someone you believe to be more spiritually mature than you. Someone you believe will keep a confidence. Because you can't be vulnerable with someone you don't fully feel safe with.

And then? Simply get to know them. Over time, open up with more of your story. Confess the ways that you've fallen short. And allow them to hold you accountable to the consequences of your choices and to pursue reconciliation in areas of brokenness.

2. BE SPECIFIC ABOUT WHAT YOU ARE CONFESSING.

Avoid vague clichés and innuendos when confessing sin. You don't need to describe every single detail, but you do need to name when, where, what, how, and why.

In my conversation with Matt, I specifically named an event that was important to me that I felt he did not show up well for. I described when and where the event took place, what he did (or really, didn't do) that was hurtful, and how and why it caused me pain. That gave us a launchpad to converse from. Matt was able to speak directly to my specific hurt, rather than having me lob emotional grenades on the table.

It's important that we get to the root of the thing beneath the thing.[23] Why do we do what we do? Only as we deconstruct the feelings, longings, and desires behind our sin or reaction can we begin to live differently moving forward.

3. FINISH WITH FORGIVENESS.

I believe the most healing part of confessing our sins to one another is hearing that we are forgiven by another brother or sister. I think this is what James was getting at: "The prayer of a righteous person is powerful and effective."[24]

To hear someone we trust and respect offer us grace in the midst of our failure reorients us to the scandalous grace of the gospel. We are reminded that our true self is not found in our mistakes, regrets, or faults. Our true self is found in the grace of Jesus Christ alone.

It is this realization that transforms us from the inside out. It is this realization that infuses us with the power and ability to become a person of forgiveness, because we grasp how we have first been forgiven.

If you are in desperate need of forgiveness today, then it's time to begin cultivating relationships that allow you to name your faults and hear the healing words "I forgive you."

If you are struggling to forgive today, then perhaps hearing that you are forgiven will begin to soften some of the callousness that's built up over the years of resentment and hurt. My friend, I want to remind you: your pain is justified. But a decision has to be made: Will you move forward in forgiveness or continue to be held back by bitterness?

I wonder what these healing words of "I forgive you" could do in your heart and soul today. You won't know unless you try.

Since discovering this practice of confession, something has shifted in my own soul. Over the years, through a lot of counseling, I've learned about the practice of differentiation. In essence, differentiation is the ability to distinguish between our emotions and the emotions that are—subtly or explicitly—being projected onto us.

In moments of intense conflict, I've had to work through my

tendency as a people pleaser to be a peacekeeper rather than a peacemaker. The distinction may not seem obvious, but it has profound implications for how I engage in conflict.

As a peacekeeper, I'm prone to . . .

> **Ignore:** I justify mistreatment with silence because it would be harder to engage in the potential conflict of disagreement.
>
> **Dismiss:** I justify mistreatment with excuses because it would be more uncomfortable to call out a hard truth than to pretend a problem doesn't exist.
>
> **Disengage:** I justify mistreatment with passive-aggressiveness because it would be more difficult to determine how I feel and clearly communicate that than to subtly or unclearly make my displeasure known.

These are all toxic tendencies that I tend to bring into conflict. However, as a peacemaker, I've learned the ability to . . .

> **Listen, listen, then speak:** Rather than justify mistreatment, I attempt to hear the other person out and typically begin my response with "I can understand how you would feel that way. I feel . . ." My wife often says, "You can't discredit how I'm feeling." There's some truth to that. But how someone is feeling may not align with reality. Still, it takes honest confession of our feelings to walk toward peace.[25]
>
> **Respect:** Rather than justify mistreatment, I respect the person I'm engaged in conflict with enough to rightly call out an offense that has taken place. I attempt to do this in a loving way that allows the person I'm conversing with to see that this rebuke is not being done on the fly or without care. Instead, I am respecting their dignity enough to call out a speck that I've seen in their eye.[26] (This presupposes I've taken the log out of my own eye!)

Believe the best: Rather than justify mistreatment, I listen for where I may have misinterpreted, misunderstood, or been misaligned in my original expectations of the person I'm in conflict with. Often, a lot of the turmoil that I'm feeling has more to do with an inner critic or cynical attitude that has developed toward the person I'm angry with than the actual offense that's occurred.

It is through these layers of emotional differentiation that I attempt to process my hurt and anger with an eye toward forgiveness and reconciliation. But this is only possible when we confess our sins to one another and genuinely seek God's healing.

We left my conversation with Matt with two choices: to punch him or to run away. One would have led to jail time, and the other would've stolen my dignity. Neither felt like a good option the longer I thought about it. (Don't worry—I was never going to punch him.)

In the moment, I was genuinely feeling inner turmoil as described earlier. And we were reaching an inflection point in this coffee shop. Any longer and Jerry Springer may have shown up on set. Eventually, I took a deep breath, which allowed me to take inventory of my internal processing. I began to come to terms with how I was trying to justify some unjustified hurt.

I had to make a choice. Peacekeeper or peacemaker?

So, eventually, I said, "Matt, I can see how some of my expectations were unrealistic, and the truth is, a lot of that was motivated by the bitterness and resentment I felt toward you and Kass for not showing up for me."

My hurt was understandable. My immature passive-aggressiveness was not.

I swallowed all of the pride, bitterness, and pain that I was sorting through and mustered up the courage to ask, "Will you forgive me?"

Asking for forgiveness is such a vulnerable position. On the one hand, if accepted, there's really nothing like it. However, if forgiveness is not extended, it can feel like a crushing blow to the soul. The point, however, is not the other person's response but our realization.

We realize our brokenness.

We realize our sinfulness.

We realize our need for grace.

We realize the ways we've fallen short.

There. That realization is what changes us from the inside out. Humility replaces haughtiness. Kindness replaces contempt. Reconciliation replaces division.

In this case, Matt graciously offered me three of the most powerful words on earth: "I forgive you."

Immediately, all the tension within me ceased. Restoration started to do its work. All the anger, hurt, and disappointment began to fade. Matt and I were ready to begin our relationship again.

But the truth is, even if he had rejected my request, I recognized that I had done the work of differentiating my responsibility from his in this painful process. I had owned what I could own. And I had done what I could to repair our relationship.

Reconciliation requires both parties to desire restoration. Forgiveness requires only one. Though I had asked Matt for forgiveness, even if he didn't forgive me, I had forgiven him. I was reintegrated in my feelings toward Matt and Kass where there had previously been a gap.

Right now, Jake, Matt, and I get together monthly for confession. We sit down at a coffee shop or breakfast place and put it all out on the table. The good, the bad, and the ugly of our souls. The resentment we're holding on to, the pain of our past, the mistakes in our relationships. We give each other space to be heard, and we listen intently. If a follow-up question needs to be asked, we ask it. If accountability needs to be instituted, we offer it. Over the years, we've added a practice at the end of our time where we say to one another,

"Matt, you're forgiven."

"Micah, you're forgiven."

"Jake, you're forgiven."

These are healing words. These are restorative words. These are words that center me back into my identity in Christ.

Meeting together forces us to—if there is any bitterness or resentment we're holding toward each other—release. It forces us to—if there is any regret, guilt, or shame we're holding toward ourselves—let go. It's become one of my favorite spaces—around the table.

My friend, there's a seat at the table for you too. The question is, who are you going to invite to it? The reality is, our table has been formed and fashioned over years of meals, fights, and laughs. Like any covenant relationship, you can't know what it's like until you've experienced it. But here—five years into these friendships—I offer a vision of the immense beauty of a relationship where one can be deeply known and loved. And I hope you are beginning to desire the same.

So, you must simply begin, wherever you are, today. As a starting point, write down the first person who comes to mind that you'd hope could be part of this safe space.

And then? Send the text. Make the call. Drive over to their house. Begin the long, slow work of developing safety and security in the context of relationship. Confess. Share. Be vulnerable. Let it all out. The worst parts of your past. The bitterness. The shame. The skeletons in your closet.

Say these confessionary words from *The Book of Common Prayer* out loud right now:

> Almighty and most merciful Father,
> we have erred and strayed from your ways like lost sheep.
> We have followed too much the devices and desires
> of our own hearts.
> We have offended against your holy laws.
> We have left undone those things which we ought to have done,
> and we have done those things which we ought not
> to have done;
> and apart from your grace, there is no health in us.
> O Lord, have mercy upon us.
> Spare all those who confess their faults.
> Restore all those who are penitent, according to your promises
> declared to all people in Christ Jesus our Lord.
> And grant, O most merciful Father, for his sake,
> that we may now live a godly, righteous, and sober life,
> to the glory of your holy name. Amen.[27]

Amen. This is a final declaration that—for those of us who are in Christ Jesus—"there is now no condemnation."[28] To you, to me, to us, Jesus says, "I forgive you." What a wonderful truth that is.

PART III

FORGIVING YOURSELF

8

EMBRACING WHAT WE AVOID

UNLESS WE'RE ABLE TO GRASP the inevitable reality of living in a broken, fallen world full of broken, fallen people who will let us down and fail us just as we let them down and fail them, we'll never be able to run the race of forgiveness.

The race is ready to be run. The question is, are you ready and willing to begin? The starting point is failure. And that's actually the best place possible to take off from.

We naturally feel uncomfortable with failure. To fail can mean many things, including a lack of success, an omission, a cessation, or a falling short.

I wonder if failure pricks at the core of our identity because God made us in his image? As a reminder, "God created mankind in his own image, in the image of God he created them; male and female he created them. God blessed them."[1]

This is where we started. But the Fall (our human condition) changed everything. Although molded by a perfect, complete, without-lack Creator, we now (rightly) see ourselves as imperfect, inadequate, incomplete, and lacking in so many ways.

I see failure as a catalytic reminder of my sinful nature. Failure shows up daily (often multiple times per day) in my life. I can't avoid it. As Paul says, "I do not understand what I do. For what I want to do I do not do, but what I hate I do."[2] Failure often feels like a weighted sandbag. The longer we hold on to it, the heavier it gets. It is a constant struggle that each of us bear.

The quote that carried me through my basketball career from grade school to college and still rings in my mind today as a pastor was this stunner from Michael Jordan, the G.O.A.T. (that's greatest of all time, thank you very much, and no, I will not debate you). "I've missed more than nine thousand shots in my career. I've lost almost three hundred games. Twenty-six times, I've been trusted to take the game-winning shot and missed. I've failed over and over and over again in my life. And that is why I succeed."[3]

Do you see it? He *embraced* failure rather than *avoiding* it.

Now, I'm not talking about an embrace, pursuit, or ambition of *moral* failure. It should never be our aim to cheat on our spouse, lie on our taxes, or steal from our business. However, I am talking about an embrace of the *reality* of failure.

Failure is inevitable. It's embedded into my life and yours. From the time we are born, we fail. And from the time we are born, we learn from failure.

Case in point: if you have kids, then you've anxiously watched your infant-turning-toddler clumsily putz around the house on their belly, then on all fours, before eventually grasping the principles of gravity, balance, dexterity, and motor skills that allows them to—AH HA!—*stand*.

But what happens next? Spoiler: they fall down. Next? They get back up. This process repeats itself over and over and over again.

From learning to walk, to riding a bike, to earning a degree, failing is part of living. The choice before us is whether we will trust in a God who works through and in spite of our failure or if we'll settle for the lie that our failure defines us.

"Mr. Davis, we need you to come to the school for a conference meeting with Micah."

"Micah?"

"Your *son*."

"Are you sure? Do you have the right person? You're talking about my son, Micah?"

"Yes, Mr. Davis. Please meet us in the classroom after school today."

It was a normal Tuesday in the life of second grade me. A few classes here, a lunch and juice box there, life was *great*.

However, on this particular day, my usual route to the bus line was interrupted by a clearly perturbed but gentle teacher of mine.

"Micah, I need you to come with me."

"Okay . . ."

As I rounded the corner into the classroom, there sat my dad with a crumpled-up piece of paper. Not *that* paper. It was the test that I had failed the week before.

Let me set the stage: a week prior, we had been given a spelling test. I have perpetually wrestled with test anxiety. I had strolled into class to take the test that I had studied rigorously for with my dad. The problem? My dad had me study the wrong spelling list. When I received the test, I didn't know any of the words and couldn't handle the weight of not knowing the answer. So, I did what any resourceful student would do—I cheated. That's right. I began looking at the test of the kid sitting to my right. *His answers don't look so good.*

I turned to the girl to my left. She was picking up on what was happening and was not happy about it. *Her answers look much better.* So, cheat away, I did.

A few days later we received our results. The guy to my right? He didn't do so hot. *Good call, Micah. He was not the right person to cheat off of.*

The girl to my left? A+. She beamed at her immaculate results. I licked my lips and readied myself for intellectual glory.

"Here you are, Micah."

At the top of my test? A gigantic (cruel, really) exaggerated "F" with a thick red circle around it. I immediately began sweating through my shirt.

What's going on?

Why's this happening?

What went wrong?

What will my classmates think?

What will my parents think?

Does she know I cheated?

A short while later, class dismissed. I tried to duck and hide on my way out into the hallway, but there wasn't a chance of escaping.

"Micah, can you stay here for a moment please?"

"Oooh! Micah's in trouble."

I sat, and my sweaty palms began to fog up the foldable desktop.

"Micah, do you want to tell me why you failed the test?"

"Because I cheated."

"That's right. Why did you cheat?"

I tried to pin it on my dad. "Because my dad gave me the wrong list."

My teacher dug in further. "But Micah, *why* did you cheat?"

The truth came out . . . "Because I didn't know the answers."

"Micah, that's not a valid excuse. You're better than this."

She proceeded to tell me that I had an additional assignment over the weekend. "This test needs to be taken to your parents, and they need to sign it so that I know they saw it. Then, I will give you a second chance to study the right list and retake the test."

The blood rushed out of my body. I couldn't think straight. *Tell my parents?* I began praying for Jesus to return.

You may be wondering why I ended up in that same teacher's classroom a few days later with my father and my test. The test that I had proceeded to take and throw away in the trash when (I thought) my teacher wasn't looking. I probably should've picked a different trash can. Nonetheless, here I was.

"Micah, why did you hide this from Mom and me?"

More truth was about to come to light. "Because I thought that if you saw that I failed, you'd be disappointed in me. I didn't want to upset you. I failed. I'm a failure."

I should clarify that up to this point, I felt zero academic pressure from my parents. They were always challenging but never overbearing. For whatever reason, I had internalized a narrative that I was only as good as my performance. However, my dad's words became a healing ointment for my soul. I ended up carrying his words throughout the rest of my academic career.

"Micah, Mom and I aren't expecting perfection from you. We're expecting your best effort. Cheating is not your best effort. I would rather you fail and try your best than take the easy route and cheat."

My line of thinking was fueled by a warped view of what success and failure are. Looking back, I can see how my primary motivators were not faith, hope, and love, but shame, fear, and doubt.

That was a long time ago, but to my dismay, I am often more like second-grade me than I like to admit—even to myself. Instead of going to God right away and confessing what I've done wrong, I convince myself that the less painful, easier route is to try to hide my sins in the proverbial classroom trash can, hoping I can somehow sneak my failure past him. Rather than leaning on a God who forgives me and subsequently learning to forgive myself, I continue on the never-ending hamster wheel of hiddenness that keeps me from discovering my true self in Christ.

The problem (and genuine grace) is, God sees everything in the trash can and still loves me anyway. God is in pursuit of reconciliation, and my propensity to hide only hinders—never helps—that pursuit.

Failure is a catalytic reminder of our sinful nature. But it doesn't have to be the narrative that rules our lives. The problem is many of us do all that we can to avoid acknowledging our starting point. I see three key motivators for why we avoid failure.

Shame

Shame is a powerful motivator to avoid failure. Shame is born out of our past. Things we've done that contribute to an aura of shame within.

Search your heart. Where might you be holding on to shame in your life? Perhaps it lies in that regret you can't shake. Maybe it's the time, or two or ten, that you were impatient with your spouse.

Perhaps it's the regretful words you said to a son or daughter in the midst of yet another fight.

As you reflect, there's a certain level of resistance that arises, isn't there? There's pain attached to our shame. To work it out, cast it off, and embrace an alternative story is difficult work.

However, it is necessary work. Why? Because if I'm experiencing shame, I'm not likely to present my true self to God.

The gift of the Cross is that the shame that's often attached to our failures was nailed there with Jesus. Here's the writer of Hebrews: "For the joy set before him he endured the cross, *scorning its shame*, and sat down at the right hand of the throne of God."[4]

Jesus is Lord not just over our failure but over our shame. And rather than avoid our shame, he invites us to offer it to him to be transformed.

Embracing failure often means encountering shame. What we do next is up to us. We can hold on to it and become perpetually anxious individuals who avoid risk and faith-filled action. Or we can be transformed by an encounter with Jesus, the Great Healer, who melts away our shame and embraces us in love, freeing us to become all we were meant to be.

Fear

I recently read an article with the clickbait title of "Top 10 Strong Human Fears." It encompassed everything from losing your freedom to disappointment and rejection.[5] But the number one fear on the list? You guessed it . . . failure.

As we know, fear and failure go hand in hand. Their symbiotic relationship is a direct driver of why we behave how we do. Fear + failure = freeze. When the fear of failure overtakes us, rather than faithfully follow God's will for our lives, we succumb to the status quo and resign ourselves to lives of comfort.

The Scriptures tend to speak directly against fear.[6]

> For God has not given us a spirit of fear and timidity, but of power, love, and self-discipline.[7]

> Have I not commanded you? Be strong and courageous. Do not be afraid; do not be discouraged, for the LORD your God will be with you wherever you go.[8]

> I have told you these things so that you will be whole and at peace. In this world, you will be plagued with times of trouble, but you need not fear; I have triumphed over this corrupt world order.[9]

Do you see the theme?

For God . . .

The Lord your God . . .

I have triumphed . . .

In other words, God has an answer to fear—and it's not an idea, theory, or policy. It's a Person. Here's God to Abraham in Genesis: "Do not be afraid, Abram. I am your shield, your very great reward."[10]

God is our shield. God is the antidote to fear. When our temptation is to succumb to fear, God asks us to submit to him. When fear runs after us, we run to God. He is our help and our strength.[11] Our fear of failure is no match for God's faithfulness.

Doubt

The temptation to doubt has been present since the beginning of time. The very first lie ever spoken was laced with doubt: "Did God really say . . . ?"[12] It was doubt that opened the door for failure to enter in the first place.

Since then, we've been perfecting our ability to doubt. Often our doubt pushes us toward isolation. It can seem easier to make sense of a reality in which we are the sole framer and builder rather than God.

But doubt isn't actually the sole owner that houses our soul. Doubt is often built on a foundation of disappointment. Think about it: What causes us to doubt? It's often prior disappointment.

Many people's doubts about God stem from prior unmet expectations.

God, why weren't you there?

God, why did she have to die?

God, why didn't you come through?

God, why did you make me this way?

God . . . WHY?

The truth that very few pastors want to share is the great mystery of life. The reality is, there is so much we don't know. But not knowing why things happen doesn't mean there isn't objective truth.

Truth is Reality. And Jesus says he is the Truth.[13] Which means Jesus is Reality. Jesus is the one we can trust.

In order for us to make peace with our propensity to fail and our need for God to rescue us, we must become aware of and attuned to our doubts. Doubt does not mean the absence of God. In fact, Jesus seems to hold space for us in our doubt.

Maybe you're familiar with what's famously known as the "great commission." It's Jesus' manifesto right before he leaves earth. It's his final instructions to his disciples. And it contains a line that the church has co-opted as its mission statement to "seek and to save the lost."[14]

But right before Jesus gives the great commission, there's this peculiar line: "Then the eleven disciples went to Galilee, to the mountain where Jesus had told them to go. When they saw him, they worshiped him; but some *doubted*."[15]

Did you catch that? Some *doubted*. The very next line is this: "Then Jesus came to them and said, 'All authority in heaven and on earth has been given to me. Therefore go and make disciples of all nations, baptizing them in the name of the Father and of the Son and of the Holy Spirit, and teaching them to obey everything I have commanded you. And surely I am with you always, to the very end of the age.'"[16]

Despite the disciples' doubt, Jesus still trusts them to carry out his mission. In a similar way, in the midst of our doubt, Jesus asks us to trust him with the great mysteries, tragedies, and sufferings of life and carry on with our faith journey. It doesn't make the unknown any less painful. However, it does make the unknown more meaningful as we trust that our Good Shepherd will meet us in the darkness and guide us.

It's belief that sets us apart from society. It's our faith that enables us to live with joy, peace, and contentment in a world of doubt. What if doubt is less of a barrier and more of an invitation? An invitation to trust God when we don't understand? To believe that he is who he says he is—despite perceived letdowns, disappointments, or silence?

What if belief—in the midst of our doubt—is the key to embracing failure rather than fearfully, shamefully, avoiding it?

Failure is inevitable. And yet, we've somehow convinced ourselves that failure is avoidable. That if we can avoid failure, then we can somehow self-actualize into an ideal self—that simply does not exist.

The words my dad offered in condolence after I failed my test echo a similar sentiment from the late, great philosopher Dallas Willard: "Grace is not opposed to effort, it is opposed to earning."[17] I can live confidently, knowing that God deserves my best effort, but also knowing my best effort will never be enough to earn the grace I have been given.

My friend, the fact of the matter is that if you're reading this, you've failed. So have I. It's inevitable. To fail is to be human. It's the starting point for all of us. If we are ever to learn how to forgive ourselves, we must begin with this truth. We cannot *earn* our way into heaven. We cannot *earn* our way into love. We cannot *earn* our way into perfection. No one can. If life is reduced to a scorecard of success versus failure, we lose. Every time.

I'm not sure if you've caught on to this, but life ends in perceived "failure." We've never found a way to beat death. It wins 100 percent of the time.

But the gospel? The Good News? The Good News is that your failure isn't final. We serve a God who took on all your failures — past, present, future — and nailed them to a cross. Three days later, he rose, conquering death and sin forever.

This gospel? This gospel is about a God who pursues us. Who freely gave what we could never earn. Who sacrificed his one and only Son so we could be reconciled to him. So we could experience everlasting life.[18]

This gospel? This gospel frees us from rules-oriented religion. We no longer have to walk on moral eggshells, because the same Spirit that raised Christ from the dead now lives in us.[19]

Instead, we're offered a new invitation. To pick up our cross and follow Jesus.[20] To practice his way. To do as he did. And to allow ourselves not to be burned out by the pressures and weight of being perfect, but to be purified by the magnificence and glory of Christ Jesus.

This is the invitation: "Come, follow me." As we follow him, we are offered a way not of forgetfulness but of forgiveness. Not of revenge but of reconciliation. We can embrace what we often avoid. Why? Because our failure isn't final — it's forgiven.

9

THE HARDEST PERSON TO FORGIVE

I CAME INTO HIGH SCHOOL a whopping five feet ten inches and 110 pounds soaking wet. If I showed you pictures, "muscular" and "athletic" wouldn't be the first two words you'd use to describe my physical stature. "Bony" and "awkward" would probably do the trick. I actually was shamefully bullied in middle school, in part due to my awkward appearance, accentuated by my no-sideburns haircut my mom loved to give me monthly in our kitchen to save money. Fun times.

So, I figured high school would be a new, fresh start. I had been recruited to attend a Christian private school in the suburbs of Nashville, Tennessee. I'll never forget meeting with Coach Drew for the first time. He told me, "We don't promise anyone anything, but we also don't hold anyone back. Three of our varsity players started as eighth graders last year. If you're good enough, I'll play you."

This was a dream to hear from a coach—especially after feeling so overlooked on my AAU team. When people ask about my high school athletic experience, it's virtually impossible to describe the unprecedented success that I was able to be a small part of for four years. This was the environment of both success—and pressure—that forged who I am today.

When I showed up for pre-season training camp the summer before my freshman year, I was thrown right into the fire of high school athletics. The person I was tasked with guarding during practice was a kid named Brandon. He would eventually go on to play collegiately. He was a gangly six-foot-three-inch point guard with the longest arms and skinniest legs you'd ever seen (skinnier than even me). Brandon was a sophomore, but he was the clear leader of the team that boasted a few of our school's most legendary players. Brandon had a charisma and charm about him that attracted anyone and everyone to him—especially girls. As an awkward fourteen-year-old who had only dipped his toes into dating, I was mesmerized by how smooth Brandon's game was on and off the court.

Brandon took me under his wing that summer, graciously inviting me to tag along with him to all of the different places he'd hang out. We started with a simple workout on a hot summer morning. And then another one in the afternoon. We'd repeat that all summer long with practices at midday. Brandon and I lived in the gym together. He crafted and shaped much of my work ethic. However, I also learned something from Brandon that would end up becoming one of the most self-destructive and debilitating features of my day-to-day life.

I learned and then ingrained negative self-talk into my head.

It started at one of those hot summer morning workouts. Brandon would shoot and make the shot, as would I. Then he'd shoot and miss. "C'mon, Brandon." Another dribble moved into a smooth three-point jump shot. Whoa, that was pretty. Then another move and the ball would bounce off his leg. "Let's goooo, B." At some point in the workout, one missed shot would turn into two, which would turn into five, and then it happened: a flurry of expletives and mumbles would arise under Brandon's breath, before finally, he'd scream, "C'mon! You suck, Brandon!" I rebounded for him, eyes wide, jarred at the level of critique and blame Brandon was putting on himself. But he was competitive. And that negative self-talk is what fueled him to become great.

I made it my mission to emulate everything Brandon did—what he said, what he ate, and how he worked on the court. I began implementing this new strategy of negative self-talk. When I missed a shot, I'd whisper, "Let's go, Mike." When I turned the ball over, I'd mumble, "C'mon, MD." And when I was really off my game, I'd let the whole gym know by yelling, "You suck, Micah!" Over time, no one became more disappointed with me than me.

This negative self-talk sent me into a spiral through my athletic career. I became my own worst critic, and I could never be good enough.

As a twenty-one-year-old, my inner life was reduced to all the parts of me that I hated, resented, and disdained. It took me years to discover and realize that the person I was struggling to forgive the most was myself. And it'd take another few years to unpack, work through, and restore the self-confidence I had lost.

This is the struggle for many of us. Forgiving those who hurt us makes sense. Forgiving God seems necessary. Forgiving life for not being fair seems wise. But forgiving ourselves? That is often where we draw the line.

In Genesis, we once again return to the story of Joseph to find a painful example of unforgiveness.

Let's set the scene: Joseph is the second youngest of twelve. He's handsome, smart, and winsome. Joseph is his father's favorite. The Scriptures don't hide this fact. "Now Israel [God's name for Jacob] loved Joseph more than any of his other sons, because he had been born to him in his old age; and he made an ornate robe for him."[1]

We're unsure of the actual Hebrew meaning for the word we translate "ornate," but a modern version could be "swaggy. Bougie. Swanky. Luxurious. Chic." This was a nice robe. A robe that matched in value the love that Jacob possessed for Joseph. And let's just say the robe doesn't win Joseph points with his ten older brothers.

But then, it gets worse. Joseph has a series of visions in which the end picture is his family bowing down to him. Joseph—in all of his seventeen-year-old pomp and ignorance—begins arrogantly sharing these visions that are keeping him up at night. If the robe incident had his brothers up to "here," then these visions took their anger over the top.

One day, while out tending to their livestock, the brothers concoct a plan to murder Joseph. They end up throwing him into a cistern (a well)—where they plan on leaving him to die. One of the brothers finally comes to his senses and convinces the other brothers not to do that. Rather, he suggests that they should profit on their brother's death. Instead of killing Joseph, they pull him up and sell him to a group of traveling slave traders. So. Much. Better.

Now enslaved, Joseph ends up in Egypt where he becomes the property of a man named Potiphar. Joseph finds favor with Potiphar and is put in charge of his entire household. All is well until Joseph catches the eye of Potiphar's wife, who attempts to seduce him into an affair. When Joseph refuses, she accuses him of making unwanted advances toward her, and Joseph is thrown into prison—unjustly—for what scholars believe to be anywhere between three to twelve years.

Once a favored son, now a desolate prisoner. Are you still with me? Almost there.

In jail, Joseph once again earns favor with those in charge. His character and ability to interpret dreams end up getting him an audience with Pharaoh—the ruler over all of Egypt. Pharaoh is so impressed with Joseph that he ends up promoting him to second-in-command. A stunning reversal.

And then . . . Joseph's brothers show up. During a continental famine, they travel all the way to Egypt in desperate search of food. Most commentators agree that it was roughly twenty-two years from the time Joseph is sold into slavery to the time he sees his brothers again.[2] As the brothers approach Joseph, they (not realizing who he is, since it's been about two decades since they last saw him) bow down before him.

Sound familiar? Joseph's vision comes to pass.

Even more miraculous than this reunion is the plot twist that takes place. When Joseph should be angry and repay his brothers for all the harm they did to him, he . . . forgives them.[3]

This is an incredible display of humility. Joseph's ability to forgive his brothers leads to an entire family-wide reunion. It seems like the quintessential happily-ever-after, right?

Until it isn't.

In fact, once Jacob—their father—dies, the brothers are terrified.[4] Why? Because Joseph was daddy's favorite, and Joseph would do anything to please his father. But Jacob's gone now, so this must be when Joseph finally executes his long-awaited revenge.

The brothers are so fearful of Joseph that they manufacture a death wish that Jacob supposedly had left for Joseph. "Now remember, Joseph, forgive your brothers. Forgive them for the way they treated you. I know it was bad, but please, for my sake, forgive them."[5]

I don't know about you, but I read this exchange and think, *Are you kidding me? Do you not know who Joseph is? He's exemplified grace and forgiveness time after time after time. He's shown the upmost character. He's embraced you, kissed you, wept over you, reconciled with you, sacrificed everything . . . for you. If he wanted to kill you, he would have!* What are these brothers thinking?

But I wonder, how often do we do the very same thing with God?

If you're a follower of Jesus, then you're probably familiar with John 3:16. It's a verse made famous by the likes of Tim Tebow and evangelicals everywhere that's been heralded as the greatest one sentence summary of the gospel in all of the Scriptures. It says, "For God so loved the world that he gave his one and only Son, that whoever believes in him shall not perish but have eternal life."[6]

This truly is a beautiful summation of the Good News of Christ.

However, many of us have heard John 3:16 so often that it's become clichéd to us. We read a familiar verse like that and think, *God, I know you love me! I know that I'm unconditionally loved! I know I'm a child of God!*

Ah, but I messed up again; will you forgive me? I know you say you will, but like, really. Will you really forgive me? Remember what the Father says, Jesus! You're supposed to forgive me! Will you really forgive me?

How often has a similar train of thought run through your mind?

You know, we go to church and hear sermon after sermon or read book after book about how the hardest thing to do in life is to forgive. And almost always, it's a conversation about how hard it is to forgive others.

We bring up Jesus' teachings concerning turning the other cheek, forgiving seventy times seven, and forgiving so that we can be forgiven.

But what if the person we struggle most to forgive is ourselves? What if the person we have the most difficult time reconciling with is the person holding this book right now?

Notice Joseph's response to his brothers: "Joseph wept."[7]

Why did he weep?

I believe Joseph wept because after all he had endured, after all he had suffered and all he had fought through to reconcile with his brothers who had betrayed him, they had the audacity to essentially say, "So, is this reconciliation for real? Or were you just faking it until Dad was gone? Because if so, please don't kill us."

At face value, that seems to be enough to make Joseph weep. But I think Joseph's tears run deeper than disappointment.

I wonder if in this moment, Joseph's first instinct is to weep because he's frustrated. Because he's deeply hurt that his brothers have not accepted—much less believed—his undeserved offer of forgiveness. Perhaps Joseph—through his tears—is communicating, "How could you not believe I forgive you? After everything I've done? How do you think this isn't real?"

This is the tragedy of unforgiveness. When we've been forgiven but have failed to forgive ourselves, not only does it hurt us, but it spits in the face of the gracious offer that's been extended to us.

I wonder if Joseph's tears for his brothers—unable to forgive themselves—are a parallel of God's tears for us, made in his image, unable to forgive ourselves. I wonder if God is up in heaven weeping over his creation that refuses to accept the undeserved gift of grace.

We could draw verse after verse that beautifully communicates God's character. He is a God who unconditionally loves us, cares for us, who watches over us, who pursues us unceasingly.[8]

And yet, the tragedy of the very same Scriptures—of our human condition—is a collective history of humanity acting out the part of Joseph's brothers, questioning God's great love for us and God routinely saying, "What must I do to prove to you that this is real?"

My friend, when you refuse to forgive yourself, you're not just hurting you. You're hurting God too! Joseph's tears in this story mirror God's tears in our story.

Joseph's brothers are unable to forgive themselves, and their perpetual angst sends them into a tailspin. They go to Egypt before hearing back from Joseph, throw themselves down before him, and declare, "We are your slaves."[9]

This is what failing to forgive ourselves does. It eats at us in the worst way. We lose sight of our identity as belonging to Christ and instead become slaves to whatever it is that's holding us down and back.

The sins of our past.

The broken relationships.

Our weaknesses.

Joseph's brothers' inability to accept forgiveness led not only to a distortion of how they viewed themselves but also how they viewed Joseph. Instead of seeing Joseph for who he really was, they cowered in fear, desperate to cling to any sense of control they felt they still had.

This doesn't have to be your story. Our God is a God of forgiveness. Dear reader . . . You. Are. Forgiven. Read that line over and over and over again. These are not my words; these are God's words.

> Forgive as the Lord forgave you.[10]
>
> In him we have redemption through his blood, the forgiveness of sins, in accordance with the riches of God's grace.[11]
>
> All the prophets testify about him that everyone who believes in him receives forgiveness of sins through his name.[12]
>
> Be merciful, just as your Father is merciful.[13]

This is who God is. And our inability to see that doesn't change reality; it only distorts God's character in our minds.

Joseph's response to his brothers is one of kindness, tenderness, and mercy—again. It's a response that flows straight from the heart of God himself. Scripture tells us, "Joseph said to them, 'Don't be afraid. Am I in the place of God? You intended to harm me, but God intended it for good to accomplish what is now being done, the saving of many lives. So then, don't be afraid. I will provide for you and your children.' And he reassured them and spoke kindly to them."[14]

My friends, this is the Good News of the gospel being preached thousands of years before Jesus ever stepped foot on earth. "You intended to harm me, but God intended it for good to accomplish what is now being done, the saving of many lives." In other words, your sinful actions—your worst mistakes, your deepest regrets, your biggest shortcomings—could not, cannot, and will not inhibit God from accomplishing what he wants to do through you.

This is the God we serve. Our God is a God who flips the script over and over and over again. He's beckoning you to shed your shame and to step into the future he has for you.

Remember, forgiveness is a practice. It's a conscious decision. A decision we have to make routinely, even for ourselves. We must choose to leave our sin, put it to death, and go another way. To return home, into the loving, warm embrace of our Father's forgiving arms.

Forgiveness is the decision God made two thousand years ago, once and for all-time through the shedding of his Son's blood on a cross. Jesus put to death the sin of all humanity—past, present, and future. As Jesus himself said, "This is my blood of the covenant, which is poured out for many for the forgiveness of sins."[15] This act was the culmination of a plan that was put in motion the moment Adam and Eve fatefully chose sin over union with God.

From that day on, what began with the question "Where are you?" led to God's unceasing pursuit of you that culminated in the blood of Jesus Christ.[16]

Many of us fall into the trap of subconsciously believing that God only loves us because Jesus died for us. Right? We might think, *God has to forgive me because I put my faith and trust in Jesus. He doesn't actually want to.*

This is what so many of us who struggle to forgive ourselves believe. We see God the Father as this ruler of the cosmos who's separate, jaded, and upset with humanity because we can never get it right or figure it out. *Thank goodness for Jesus, because if it weren't for Jesus, God would hate us.*

In fact, perhaps you're reading this today and you think that God does hate you. You're grateful for Jesus' sacrifice that's saved you, but you've yet to place your faith and trust in a God who loves you. Does this resonate with you?

Here's the deal: we can forgive ourselves because God forgives us. God does not love us because Jesus died for us; Jesus died for us because God loves us. Such a subtle shift, but one that will change your perspective forever.

Read John 3:16 through *that* lens! "For God so loved the world . . ."

He—God—so loved the world that he gave (or he sent, or he offered) his one and only Son, that whoever believes in him shall not perish but have eternal life.

Our God is a God who holds the ultimate trump card, the ace in the hole. It's his Son, Jesus. God turned an instrument of pain into a pillar of new life. God turned death itself on its head and fashioned resurrected life. This is the gospel. Good News for all who repent and believe.

The apostle John wrote, "If we confess our sins, he is faithful and just and will forgive us our sins and purify us from all unrighteousness."[17]

He is faithful and just to forgive.

The beautiful, redemptive arc of the Scriptures—and of life—is a narrative of individuals who repeatedly have their messy lives turned into messages of redemption. From Abraham to David, from Rahab to Daniel, from Peter to Paul, from my dad to me. We see God routinely taking past actions or habits and transform them.

Instead of speaking words of condemnation over myself, I now embrace words of hope, joy, peace, life, and love that have been spoken over me.

I never would've been able to step into my role as a teacher of Scripture if I first did not come to believe the message that I preach. Words about ultimate forgiveness that I—to my core—*believe*.

So, how do we go about forgiving the hardest person to forgive? How do we forgive *ourselves*?

1. DECISION

In order to get out from underneath the grip of self-hate and regret, we have to make a choice, a decision. First, to see God for who he really is. What you believe about God determines everything. A. W. Tozer said it this way: "What comes into our minds when we think about God is the most important thing about us."[18]

What comes into your mind when you think about God? Is he the God of John 3:16—the God who loves you unconditionally and with reckless abandon? Is he a God who pursues you over and over again—even when you reject him, even when you curse him, even when you deny him?

My friend, God is after you. Not in a gotcha, you're caught, shame-ridden way, but in a way that beckons and yearns for you to come out of hiding. In the loving arms of a Savior, and in the presence of brothers and sisters in the faith, you are safe.

He's there. He loves you. He sees you.

For many of us, we see God the way Joseph's brothers saw Joseph. We see him as the forgiver with conditions. We think that if we don't meet his standards, then he won't forgive us.

We have to make a decision to see God for who he really is. But then we also must make a decision to see ourselves as we really are, in Christ.

Toward the end of my athletic career, I began to spend a lot of time in counseling unwinding all of the negative self-talk that had come to define how I saw myself. My counselor had me do an exercise of walking through different passages of Scripture that spoke to identity. Eventually, we came up with this list below. I read this list aloud over myself for the better part of two years, seeking to replace the negative self-talk with positive identity traits regarding who I am in Christ. I realized that I am . . .

> a conqueror (Romans 12:21)
>
> chosen (Matthew 22:14)
>
> valued (1 Peter 1:18)
>
> loved (John 15:9)
>
> redeemed (Psalm 107:2)
>
> cared for (Psalm 112:7)
>
> disciplined (Proverbs 3:11)
>
> able to endure (James 1:3; Romans 5:3-4)

My friend, dig into the Scriptures. Read God's Word. Talk to him—ask him to reveal his true self to you and to reveal your true self to you. Make your own list of who he says you are. Let his truth wash over you. And then make the decision to believe in his character. To trust that he is who he says he is. And that *you* are who he says you are.

2. SUBMISSION

After we make a decision to believe God loves us and that we are forgiven, we must then enter a posture of submission.

Joseph's brothers came before Joseph and bowed before him saying, "We are your slaves!" But Joseph was upset because he didn't want slaves; he wanted *brothers*. God doesn't want slaves; he wants sons and daughters.

Joseph's brothers weren't coming to Joseph out of reverence; they were coming to him out of fear. Jesus doesn't want us to fear him;

he wants us to revere him. Joseph's brothers were willing to offer their obedience to Joseph in exchange for his mercy. Jesus desires for us to offer our allegiance to him because we have already been offered mercy. It's a transformational distinction, and the difference is freedom. He gave up everything; he offered up himself as a ransom so that instead of being owned by sin, shame, guilt, or regret, we can find freedom in forgiveness.

Eventually, I traded in a basketball for a microphone. There's no better place to be than on a stage with hundreds of people staring at you (again, sarcasm, friends). I had to unlearn and relearn that my worth and identity were not tied to positive feedback. I did not need praise and affirmation to be obedient to what Jesus had asked me to do. I had to learn to let go of who I thought other people *wanted* me to be and embrace who God had *called* me to be.

My point is, my career as a pastor has been more enjoyable not because it's been less difficult or I've been more successful, but because my identity is no longer primarily rooted in my performance but in my position. I am not defined by what I do. I am defined by who I am. And who I am is a son of God. An heir to his Kingdom. A co-ruler and co-conqueror with Jesus. These are not truths I simply believe, but live. Certainly not perfectly but consistently.

You, too, are so much more than your performance. You are a person—made in the image of God. A God who loves you more than you could ever dare dream, who accepts you more than you could ever dare hope, and who forgives you more than you could ever dare imagine.

3. INTENTION

Once we've made a conscious decision to see God and ourselves rightly, and once we've entered into a posture of reverent submission, only then are we in a place to live out transformed intentions.

We are sinful people who fall short often. Whether we're willing to admit it or not, our intentions are not always good, pure, selfless, or kind.

But as we make the conscious decision to see God for who he really is, and as we make the deliberate choice to submit ourselves to him, he begins to redeem our lives for good.

What Satan meant for evil, God used for good.

What we meant for evil, God used for good.

What lying, stealing, or cheating in your past meant for evil, God can use for good.

Our God is a God who takes our oft-sinful intentions and turns them into glorious exhibitions of his character, might, power, and mercy.

For years I was haunted by words. The negative script I learned, spoke, and lived crushed me, and eventually I became a shell of myself. But over the last decade-plus, I've witnessed God flip the script in my life. Words used to haunt me. Now words are my vocation. Words spoken over me brought destruction and pain. Now I write words that bring hope and healing. Words lived inside of me that brought immense shame. Now I speak words that bring freedom. Talk about a plot twist!

Only God could take a young man enslaved by words and use them as the vehicle to bring me and others closer to himself. All glory, all honor, and all praise to him, as per usual.

Perhaps the most tragic part of Joseph's story isn't him being sold into slavery, having his character assassinated by Potiphar's wife, or being unjustly thrown into prison.

The most tragic part of Joseph's story is his brothers' unwillingness to forgive themselves. They simply could not wrap their head around the mercy that Joseph was showing them. They could not understand how—despite their worst mistakes, their horrible intentions, their massive failings—their brother and their God could forgive them.

And you know what? Often this is the greatest misfortune of *our* lives.

Despite all that God does to show us over and over again his kindness, his goodness, his gentleness, and his mercy, there are times when—for whatever reason—we won't accept it. However, through Joseph's response to his brothers, we are offered an echo of God's heart. Joseph says, "'So then, don't be afraid. I will provide for you and your children.' And he reassured them and spoke kindly to them."[19]

In your worst moment . . .

In your darkest hour . . .

At your lowest low . . .

You are forgiven.

God knows your intentions weren't good, but his always are. God knows that your motives weren't pure, but his always are. The invitation before us is to stop beating ourselves up, making excuses, and holding ourselves captive and imprisoned in shame.

Jesus Christ sacrificed everything for *you*. He gave up everything for you. He loves you. And he—like Joseph—continually reassures us and speaks kindly to us. He is the great provider and sustainer.

Everett Worthington—the guru on forgiveness—suggests a helpful process for forgiving yourself that is absolutely beautiful.[20] He writes that we mustn't forgive ourselves irresponsibly. It is not forgiveness to ourselves—just like to others—if we let ourselves off the hook or forgive and forget. There is a *process* to engage in.

First, we must receive God's forgiveness. We must make amends and come to a place of security in who God is.

Next, we should move to any relationships that have been affected by our poor decisions. How do we initiate reconciliation? We confess, repent, and ask for forgiveness. If the damage is unrepairable, we learn from our past mistakes and discern ways that we can be a guide for people behind us to avoid similar consequences.

Throughout this process, we must be patient and gracious to ourselves. Often, in the rehabilitation process of our self-image, we tend to be hyper-critical and instead of feeling healthy remorse, we fall into unhealthy shame. This perfectionistic standard will only delay our progress as we become captive to unrealistic expectations. Remember, the decision to forgive is instant, but the process of building back trust and healing—even with yourself—takes time.

After working through this process yourself, consider inviting in a trusted mentor, counselor, or friend and communicating what you did wrong. But don't stop there. Share why you've repented or committed to turning around and living a different way, and how you will live into this new reality of forgiveness. Accountability can help rebuild your self-worth and self-acceptance.

God loves you. God forgives you. Often these truths are half-heartedly said, and the weight and power of these words is lost. But don't miss this.

God *loves* you.

God *forgives* you.

Now, the invitation before you and me is to forgive ourselves. To make a conscious decision to trust his character, to offer ourselves in submission to his love, mercy, and grace, and to walk intentionally in step with the God who sees, knows, and loves you just as you are.

PART IV

FORGIVING

GOD

10

THE BIG QUESTION

RYAN COULD NOT STOP CRYING.

It was cold. Too cold to be outside. But that's where we found ourselves: five houses down from mine, on a back porch, as Ryan wept into his lap. We'd been classmates and neighbors for almost four years at this point. For the last two years, he had joined me as a high school basketball teammate. Most of his family had come to faith at our church. And still, I'd never seen him show emotion like this.

I breathed heavily and slowly, watching the cool air make the invisible visible.

It seemed like a perfect descriptor of Ryan's life. The tension between his parents—which for so long had remained mostly imperceptible to any on the outside—had spilled over publicly. They had just delivered the news. They would be pursuing a divorce.

I sat there, trying to conjure up words of comfort and condolence.

"Ryan, I know what this feels like. I know what it's like to watch your dad walk out on you. I know what it's like to feel abandoned. I know what it's like to be hurt and afraid."

Eventually, Ryan's body began to still—surely tired from exerting so much energy crying in the cold. After a few sniffles, he looked at me and asked a singular question: "Where the hell is God?"

Can a God who allows suffering be trusted?

That's the big question, isn't it?

I mean, sure, we all (hopefully) have the gist by now that humans are imperfect and make mistakes. That failure is inevitable. That forgiveness is a must if we are to maintain relationship with people who constantly—unintentionally or purposefully—break our bond.

But what about God?

Often, in times of desperation, need, or fear, we turn to God and await a miraculous rescue. Isn't that what God is supposed to do?

God is love. God is perfection. God is whole. And he loves *us*, right?

So how do we forgive him when it feels like he's absent? Silent? Nowhere to be found? It feels right to pin any sort of pain on a seemingly pain-free God.

If God is all-powerful, why doesn't he step into my situation?

If God is all-knowing, why doesn't he stop the evil before it comes?

If God is all-present, why doesn't he make himself known to me?

These are all good, difficult questions that followers of Jesus have been asking for millennia. In fact, these questions are not evidence of doubt, but of *faith*. It takes faith to examine our beliefs and ask God our honest questions about suffering.

There is a wide swath of thinking that seems to pit doubt and faith against each other. But the Scriptures give a lot of room for doubt.

In the Gospel of Luke, we see doubt bubble to the surface in both Zechariah's and Mary's responses to an angel's announcement about a seemingly miraculous birth. "How can I be sure of this? I am an old man and my wife is well along in years,"[1] Zechariah questioned. "'How will this be,' Mary asked the angel, 'since I am a virgin?'"[2]

In the Gospel of John, Andrew seems to doubt Jesus' ability to provide food for the over-five-thousand hungry people in their midst. "Here is a boy with five small barley loaves and two small fish, but how far will they go among so many?"[3]

Even the great commission, which often is used (rightfully) as a rally cry for followers of Jesus to do the will of God, begins like this: "Then the eleven disciples went to Galilee, to the mountain where Jesus had told them to go. When they saw him, they worshiped him; but some *doubted*."[4]

Let's begin by normalizing your feelings of doubt. The very room these words are being typed in is where I laid flat on my face in April of 2023, crying out to God, wondering where in the world he was. A year prior, we had sensed the Spirit calling us to step out and plant a new community of faith inside the loop of Indianapolis. In April we had a growing church that was meeting monthly on Sunday nights with no place to call home. We had been turned down by twenty-four different venues. After that last no, I was on the verge of giving up. Immense doubt was weighing me down. I felt like God didn't care. And deeper still, I felt like I may have misheard God.

So, if you've ever felt hurt, let down, dismissed, abandoned, or forgotten by God, know that you are not alone. In fact, for all of time, people have been trying to discern and uncover the ways of God—his presence and absence, his nearness and distance, his voice and silence.

However, the fact of the matter is that on this side of heaven God's ways remain a mystery. As he says to the prophet Isaiah, "'For my thoughts are not your thoughts, neither are your ways my ways,' declares the Lord."[5]

How, then, are we to reconcile with a God who has seemingly let us down? How do we forgive God?[6] We begin by looking to God himself . . .

God the Son had prayers that went unanswered.

God the Son felt abandoned by God the Father.

God the Son endured God the Father's silence and seeming absence.

How about Jesus' prayer in the garden of Gethsemane on the eve of his crucifixion? "My Father, if it is possible, may this cup be taken from me."[7] In other words, "Father, if I don't have to die, please don't make me." That prayer went unanswered.

Or how about Jesus on the cross? "About three in the afternoon Jesus cried out in a loud voice, *'Eli, Eli, lema sabachthani?'* (which means 'My God, my God, why have you forsaken me?')."[8]

This is God asking God, "Where are you?"

And there's . . . silence.

My point in sharing all of this is that our propensity to argue that God is merely someone who "doesn't understand" or "is aloof" or "doesn't care" seems to not hold its weight.

We are talking about a God who "gave his one and only Son"[9] to die so that you and I could live. A God who at some level has experienced unanswered prayer, rejection, silence, abandonment . . . and yet, was able to faithfully declare, "Yet not as I will, but as you will."[10]

So, as we attempt to reconcile with God, let's enter in with a posture of humility, recognizing that we are talking to and about Someone who understands—with holes in his hands as proof.

I know this doesn't directly answer Ryan's question. So, let's turn our attention to unanswered prayer, silence, and the absence of God.

It was a Wednesday night. I stayed late at the office because I had life group to lead for my high school guys. A short commute over to the host house, some knockout on the basketball court, and then into our discussion for the evening in the basement. This was my routine—every Wednesday—for four years. Over time, that basement became holy ground.

For a few weeks, Paul had been noticeably absent from the group. When Paul did show up again, he didn't seem like himself. He was always a quiet kid. Particularly shy. But the last few weeks were different. There was a closed-offness to Paul that hadn't been present before. Anytime I asked, he didn't give a reason.

It was only after a group member's mom—who also had cancer—told me that Paul's mom was battling cancer that everything started to click. The next week, I made a point to bring it up to Paul.

"Hey, man, heard about your mom. I'm so sorry. How's she doing?"

Paul went on to tell me that she was okay and that she'd be living in Wisconsin for the next three months to experiment with an aggressive form of chemo that at least gave her a shot to beat the disease taking over her body. For those months, Paul saw his mom only on a semi-regular basis. But every week that he showed up to the group, we'd pray for healing—for both moms.

Over time, the other high schooler's mom began to recover and announced she was cancer free. We were overcome by joy and celebration as we praised God for the healing that had taken place.

But Paul's mom grew worse. So we prayed harder.

A few months later, I got a call from Paul's dad. "Micah, it's Jim. Jordan's not doing well. She's home, and they've only given her a few days at best. Would you come over and pray with us?"

Their house was down the street from church, but the drive felt hours long. I turned over a hundred times what I might say, how I might pray, and how I might avoid showing the same discontent, frustration, and anger that Jim and Paul were expressing toward God for their present circumstance.

When I arrived at their house, we prayed. I turned to the only prayer that would come to mind—the Lord's Prayer—and asked for God's will to be done. I sat with Paul and Jim in silence, watching Jordan struggle to breathe, listening to the few thoughts they were turning over in their heads, and then left.

The next time I saw Jim and Paul was a week later in the church office as we prepared for Jordan's funeral. Sitting with their family, Jim and Paul appeared zapped of all the strength they had exuded during the last few months. They were empty, cold, and bitter. How could they not be? Their wife and mom had been taken from them. And in that office space, the honest questions came.

"Micah, we prayed and prayed for healing. Why didn't God listen? Where is he? Why did this have to happen? How come our prayers didn't work?"

I sat there, attempting to concoct an answer of hope, but in all honesty, I was wondering the same thing. I couldn't help but think about the other group member's mom who had experienced healing. Whose family got to stay together. Whose life got to go on.

Why her? Why now?

I started thinking about all the people in the world who—at that moment—were enduring similar, if not greater, forms of suffering and crying out to God. *God, where are you? Are you listening? Do you even care?*

Unanswered prayer can feel painful and disorienting. There are a whole host of reasons—that we are unaware of—for why God is seemingly absent, distant, or silent in particular situations. Why he doesn't intervene in the ways we hope for. Why we don't always see him appear.

There is a genuine mystery to the physical and spiritual workings of this world that we might never fully understand. As I once heard Dr. Rich Plass comment, "We must honor the reality of the complexity of the human soul."[11]

The questions that Jim and Paul asked me—"Why didn't God listen? Where is he? Why did this have to happen? How come our prayers didn't work?"—still haunt me.

My honest answer is that I don't know. That may be unsettling for you, but in these moments of mystery, we have a choice to make: either we can press into God's character, or we can retreat into cynicism.

Amid the complexity of life, I've had to diligently submit my doubts to Jesus in exchange for peace that surpasses understanding.

The underlying root of anger toward a person or group of people—as an image bearer or image bearers of God—is often a profound sense of indignation toward God himself.

God, how could you let this happen?

God, why me?

God, where are you?

Once again, many of us who have grown up in the church—or even outside the church—have been given little room to explore complex emotions toward the God we call "Father."

For those of us with any sort of father wound, how we relate to God—as trusted confidant, protector, provider, friend, and

Father—can be heavily informed by our relationship, or lack thereof, with our biological father.

For years, I wrestled with feelings of abandonment and rejection by God the Father because of my experience of being abandoned and rejected by my earthly father figures. The truth is, healing and building back trust—with my Father and father(s)—has not been a linear process. It's come in waves, as I've navigated seasons of joy and grief, faith and doubt, intimacy and distance. And yet, as time has passed, I've begun to recognize that I am the one who is changing. God never does. This has brought me peace and hope that—regardless of where I am emotionally, spiritually, or mentally—God is present, near, and available. How couldn't he be? He is unchanging and ever loving.

King David offers us further insight into the intimate relationship we are able to cultivate with God as Father. The capacity of grace and patience that God holds for us is overwhelming.

Here's the psalmist in Psalm 89: "[David] will call out to me, 'You are my Father, my God, the Rock my Savior.'"[12] David's foundational trust in God as his Father affords him the safety to be vulnerable in expressing his emotions to God.

Recognize this one? "My God, my God, why have you forsaken me? Why are you so far from saving me, so far from my cries of anguish? My God, I cry out by day, but you do not answer, by night, but I find no rest."[13] That's right. The anguish, distance, and separation that Jesus felt from God the Father on the cross? His language for that experience comes from David.

Perhaps you've felt ashamed of your anger toward God. But what if that shame has kept you from expressing the feelings you need to express in order to heal? My friend, God invites and welcomes your anger.

So, yell! Scream! Kick! Shadowbox in your prayer room. Do what you need to (righteously) to cathartically process all the rage pent up within. If God really is who he says he is, then he can handle our grief, disappointment, and frustration.

All throughout the Psalms, we are given examples of wrestling with frustration, confusion, anger, and doubt.[14] David knows what it's like to wrestle with God. To feel his absence, his distance, and his silence. But . . . David understands the key to navigating his intense feelings with God. Namely, like Jesus, David does not give up on God the Father. He keeps pursuing, he keeps seeking, he keeps knocking, as God does with us. And in that pursuit, further intimacy, deeper trust, and greater joy is found.

Many of us stop reading after David's anguishing cry in Psalm 22:1-2. But keep reading. In the next line, he writes, "Yet you are enthroned as the Holy One; you are the one Israel praises. In you our ancestors put their trust; they trusted and you delivered them. To you they cried out and were saved; in you they trusted and were not put to shame."[15]

Just as David offers us a vision for intimate expression of anger toward God, so, too, does he offer us a vision for hopeful faith in God despite our lack of understanding.

Let's revisit one of my favorite quotes: "There is a God and you aren't him."[16] When I consider these words, I am reminded that—as much as I'd like to be—I am not in control. I am not the captain of my ship. I am not the maker of my way.

God is. God hears our cries and listens and longs for us to run into his safe, loving arms. He sees you. He cares for you. He hurts with you. Sin, death, violence, cancer . . . he detests all of it. And one day, he's going to set everything right.

"Well, that's not fair. God needs to pay for all the evil he's allowed!" You might want this to be true. But the Good News of the gospel is that he *has* paid the price. Christ's death, burial, resurrection, ascension, and eventual return are the currency for eternal restoration and reconciliation to take place.

Jesus took on your sin; your shortcomings; and your evil thoughts, words, and actions. He took on the weight of all humanity's sin.

And he conquered its inevitable consequence—death—opening the door to a new reality, a new story to be written.

Your situation might be difficult. Your pain might be justified. But God is not to blame. God is the one offering the only way out of this vicious cycle called sin. So cast your cares, your hurts, your pain, and your wrath onto him. He can handle it. In fact, he already has. Two thousand years ago, naked, scorned, shamed, and nailed to a tree.

Forgive him. He's already forgiven you.

Perhaps you've squared away your personal beef with God. But you can't forgive him for allowing suffering on a global scale. How could a loving, compassionate, just God allow sex slavery, ethnic genocide, child hunger and poverty, and natural disasters to happen on his watch? How are we to forgive a God who seems to be absent while an entire human race hungers and thirsts for equity?

Often, the loudest critics and opponents of a suffering God are those of us who have not experienced suffering ourselves. It's ironic that we denounce God on the basis of global suffering when many of us are so privileged and unknowingly contribute to said suffering.

Case in point, check the shoes on your feet right now. My guess is, they are from a big-name brand. Almost all of those brands rate as "not good enough" in their labor conditions, fashion transparency index, and workplace code of conduct.[17] We all have blind spots—God alone sees those who are suffering.

For all of time, God has cared. In fact, it's through individuals facing suffering that he's often done his most powerful work.

The Israelites were an oppressed people whom God delivered. He brought Jesus into the world through them. The early church was an oppressed group, brutalized and murdered for the Christian faith, that brought the hope of Jesus to the masses.

Many others of us who are wrestling with this question about justice are, in fact, suffering. It is here that we see two camps diverge. There are those whose faith is shipwrecked on the iceberg of disbelief in a God who seems disproportionately cruel or apathetic. But there are also those who cling to the ultimate promise given by the Suffering Servant himself: that one day Jesus will return to restore all things.

This, of course, can't become a platitude pitched softly into the abyss of human hopelessness. Thankfully, it's not. There is teeth to this Truth. Not just teeth, but feet, and hair, and a face, and scars. His name is Jesus. He stands in overwhelming solidarity with the suffering. The prophet Isaiah calls him "a man of suffering."[18] In other words, this is no God who merely talks the talk. He walks the walk.

If God is who he says he is—the King of Kings and Lord of Lords, the Creator, Sustainer, and Maker of all things, the Redeemer of all that is evil into all that is good, true, and beautiful—then does it not make sense that suffering becomes a vital avenue to experiencing loving union with him?

The apostles bleed this truth all over the pages of the Scriptures.[19] On and on I could go, but the point is that the journey toward new life is often through the valley of the shadow of death.

We follow our Savior's lead, cry our tears, bear the wounds that are inflicted upon us, and, perhaps most beautifully and prophetically, we share our scars with those around us as evidence of Christ's transformative, redemptive power.

In the end, he wins.

God is beckoning you to return to him. Throw all the blame, all your pain, and all your frustration onto him. This is the necessary work of forgiveness. As the Catholic mystic Fr. Ronald Rolheiser says, there are four exercises of forgiveness that we must traverse if we are to redeem our past and become people of love in this life. We must forgive other people, ourselves, life for not being fair, and God for not saving us from it all.[20]

Please know, there is grace in the process of grieving and forgiving the hurt you've experienced. But the invitation remains to do the work.

In order to move forward, we must answer the big question of life: Where is God? We must forgive God for the complexity of the question in the first place. It was never our burden to carry. The truth is he's right here: near, present, and attuned to your pain. Invite him in. He understands.

It is here that I'd like to make a note on church hurt. The church—being the bride of Christ—can get closely intertwined into the conversation about anger toward God. This may not be your story. Or perhaps you find yourself in the broader camp of "I like your Christ, but I do not like your Christians."[21] Either way, I want to specifically address those of you who have endured church hurt.

How do we forgive the church? How do we forgive the place that was supposed to keep us safe, welcome us in, and offer us a home to belong when it does the exact opposite?

As I've already mentioned, I've experienced my fair share of church hurt.

I've faced the full gamut of people being people. I've been cussed out on the phone by a raging parent for attempting to hold their daughter accountable. I've had leaders enthusiastically sign up to lead and serve, only to abandon ship soon after. I've had my words and actions picked apart in an effort to build cases against my integrity. I've been gaslit, strung along, and outright denied opportunity by leaders ahead of me.

I've witnessed double standards and hypocrisy at different levels of organizational leadership. I've watched countless coworkers be sidelined, shamed, and silenced under the guise of protection of the broader institution. I've had numerous conversations with individuals who have left church leadership, the church itself, or following Jesus altogether because of painful past experiences.

In light of this, a question I am often asked is how I'm not jaded toward God or the church. You'd think that after enduring multiple massive church scandals, it'd be easy to blame the church.

And there certainly have been seasons when I have.

God, how could you?

God, why?

God, make this right!

I've prayed Psalm 109 countless times in righteous anger toward some of the appalling, cowardly acts I've seen done "in the name of the Lord." It grieves my heart to no end.

But, like David, I've come to a place of trust and hope in the Lord. Over time, I've been able to differentiate how the hurt that I've experienced has come not from the Lord but from people acting in his name. And while that is deeply painful, it is different. The church as a whole has not wounded me; people in the church have wounded me. I can't blame the church, because I've seen God—time and time again—use what Satan meant for evil, for good. I've seen beauty come from ashes. I've seen restoration take place. I've seen wrongs made right. Every time, it is a glimpse of heaven.

Those experiences don't make past hurts any less painful or wrong. But God's faithfulness, mercy, and kindness shine brightest in the darkest spaces.

In the suffering of church hurt, I have found, over and over, a God who sees me. Who cares for me. And who cares for his church. We mustn't forget this, my friends. It is God's church. Our job is to be faithful to the calling of building his church, but he is the one who makes it happen. This is Good News, because even when we fail, God does not.

I have found no other avenue to bring healing, hope, and restoration on earth as it is in heaven than the local church. Our church here in Indy is not perfect by any stretch of the imagination, but we've made it our ambition to become, in part, a haven for broken people. That piece of our mission statement was born out of deep pain in my past. But it's a past I wouldn't trade for the world, because God has redeemed it, forgiven it, and restored my present. My future is secure in him.

Forgiveness is possible when we realize that we're not in control of the church. God is. The local church is worth fighting for. It's worth belonging to. And so, if you find yourself in a season of church hurt, please take time to heal. But do your part to heal, and then return.[22] Try again. Root yourself in a community. You will risk being hurt. And you probably will be hurt again. Failure is inevitable. But belonging, community, family, is just on the other side. When it goes right, it's but a taste of what is to come.

I was rewatching the award-winning film *Interstellar* recently and was struck by the poem that Professor Brand (Michael Caine) recited throughout. It's original to a Welsh Poet, Dylan Thomas. Thomas wrote the tragic poem for his father while on his deathbed. Its words are striking. Our natural tendency is to, as Thomas brilliantly writes, "rage, rage against the dying of the light." In other words, it's natural for us to become angry, bitter, and upset at life's unfairness. At the end, we have an opportunity to look back and to see a dark, cold, cruel world.

Or we can "go gentle into that good night."[23] In other words, we can—over the course of time—work out with God all the unfairness, injustice, and pain that we've endured. We can forgive the ways that we wanted him to show up that he didn't and the pain that we wanted him to take away that he hasn't. We can find meaning when we recognize that we serve a God who suffered along with us and will bring about restoration. Embracing this ultimate reality brings healing to our present reality.

We can get swept up in the pain and problems of this world. Or we can capture a bigger, better story. A story where Jesus—God incarnate—is who he says he is. The resurrection and the life. And we can better still find God's presence, God's goodness, and God's mercy redeeming it all.

11

A FORGIVING FUTURE IN A FAILING PRESENT

WE SERVE A GOD WHO IS intimately familiar with our pain. A God who knows and understands the difficulty of enduring painstaking silence, distance, or absence. Still, in a fallen, broken present, what do we do with sin? The most painful parts of life? How do we respond to the injustices of this world? And how do we usher in a forgiving future?

This is where many of us come to the end of ourselves. Where all the existential questions of life come to the surface:

God, why do bad things happen to good people?

God, why are some people dealt such a bad hand in life?

God, WHY?

Often the pain and heaviness of a failing present can deter us from ever desiring—much less working toward—a better, redeemed, forgiving future.

But what if we've got it backward? In Jesus, we find a Wounded Healer. Our past is redeemed by the Suffering Servant himself who first forgave us, bearing all the sins and evil of the world on his shoulders. In light of this, what if we're misdirecting our disappointment, hurt, and anger? What if instead of putting God on trial, we're the ones on trial? What if rather than aiming these questions at God, we aim them at ourselves?

Micah, why do you do bad things?

Micah, why do you take advantage of others?

Micah, WHY?

What then? What if—rather than us forgiving God—we look at his nature as a *forgiving* God and all the ways we've fallen short?

What if—in a world filled with violence, injustice, and evil—we're the ones on the stand, having to answer for the ways we've contributed to our failed reality?

The prophet Micah offers a vision that encapsulates us being on trial in Micah 6. "Listen to what the LORD says: 'Stand up, plead my case before the mountains; let the hills hear what you have to say. Hear, you mountains, the LORD's accusation; listen, you everlasting foundations of the earth. For the LORD has a case against his people; he is lodging a charge against Israel.'"[1]

In the American court of law, a defendant is innocent until proven guilty. But what do you do when your prosecutor is the all-knowing, all-powerful, ever-present God? What defense do you have?

Short answer? None. And God knows this. So he lays his case before the people of Israel: "My people, what have I done to you?

How have I burdened you? Answer me. I brought you up out of Egypt and redeemed you from the land of slavery. I sent Moses to lead you, also Aaron and Miriam. My people, remember what Balak king of Moab plotted and what Balaam son of Beor answered. Remember your journey from Shittim to Gilgal, that you may know the righteous acts of the LORD."[2]

There it is. The sins of Israel laid bare. Eight hundred years of history—receipts, as we like to call them—are submitted for evidence.

God is effectively saying, "Israel, I rescued you from slavery. I gave you a leader. In fact, I gave you a leadership team! I've redeemed and saved you over and over again. Remember Balak? Remember how you chose to give in to the pleasures of a foreign king's idols instead of trusting the promises of the Lord your God? Remember your journey from Shittim to Gilgal? You know, the journey from the wilderness into the promised land? How I carried you and saw you through your wandering in the desert? How I raised up Joshua to lead and guide you into this land that I promised your ancestors Abraham, Isaac, and Jacob? Remember?"

Understand that this is not just a trial of Israel. This is a trial of the human condition. At the basis of disobedience, disruption, and destruction in our failed present is forgetfulness. We *forget*.

Our memory is lost when it comes to God's grace, provision, kindness, and mercy toward us. In turn, we end up living out of a posture of fear for what is rather than faith for what's to come. We live out of greed rather than generosity. We live out of violence rather than peace. When sin entered the world, it was forgetfulness that served as the gateway: "Did God really say . . . ?"[3]

In Hebrew the word "forget" is *shâkach*. And *shâkach* translates as "to ignore, to wither, to cease to care [about], to make or cause to forget."[4] This kind of forgetting is not passive. It is a deliberate decision to remove the Lord from our mind. This word—*shâkach*—shows up at least one hundred times in the Old Testament alone.[5] To name a few . . .

Only be careful, and watch yourselves closely so that you do not *forget* the things your eyes have seen or let them fade from your heart as long as you live.[6]

Be careful not to *forget* the covenant of the LORD your God that he made with you; do not make for yourselves an idol in the form of anything the LORD your God has forbidden. For the LORD your God is a consuming fire, a jealous God.[7]

You have *forgotten* God your Savior; you have not remembered the Rock, your fortress.[8]

This is what the Sovereign LORD says: "Since you have *forgotten* me and turned your back on me, you must bear the consequences of your lewdness and prostitution."[9]

On and on I could go, but the point remains: it is within this environment of forgetfulness that injustices grow and fester. God is putting that forgetfulness onto the witness stand as one piece of evidence for why the world is not as it should be.

The prophet Micah—on behalf of the people—responds, "With what shall I come before the LORD and bow down before the exalted God? Shall I come before him with burnt offerings, with calves a year old? Will the LORD be pleased with thousands of rams, with ten thousand rivers of olive oil? Shall I offer my firstborn for my transgression, the fruit of my body for the sin of my soul?"[10]

Micah is on the hot seat, and he knows it. Here he is, wrestling and contending for humanity, and essentially, he throws his hands up . . . "Guilty! Guilty! Yes, we're guilty, God! So what do you want us to do?"

Can you sense the bitterness and exasperation in Micah's voice? *God, what do you want from me? You want a burnt offering? You want a thousand rams or ten thousand rivers of olive oil?*

How about this last chilling line . . . "the fruit of my body for the sin of my soul?"

Micah's not looking for restoration—returning humanity to its original, beautiful, *forgiven*, perfect state—he's looking for reparation.

How do I pay for this, God? How do I fix this? What do you need? An offering? God, should I give you my firstborn? My own son?

How often have we found ourselves in this position, bartering with God? Trying to offer the fruit of our body for the sin of our soul? Trying to reason with God in exchange for our salvation? Trying to convince God we're worth forgiving? Attempting to earn our way into heaven?

Oh, but God, I really am a good person. Look at what I've done. You want me to point out that one nice thing I did last week? The thousand good things I did last year? The ten thousand great things I've done over the course of my life, God? Is that enough?

This is Micah conceding. *You win, God. None of our good deeds will be enough to earn your forgiveness. We're . . . guilty.*

In Micah 6, with humanity on trial, Micah has pleaded our case. Everything's been said . . . and then, the air gets sucked out of the room. "He has shown you, O mortal, what is good. And what does the LORD require of you? To act justly and to love mercy and to walk humbly with your God."[11]

We often fail to understand the seismic decree this is.

Up to this point, over hundreds of years, Israel forgot, God remembered, Israel forgot, God remembered. And so, to curb their forgetfulness, Moses—through God—had instituted 613(!) commands to keep as they sought to follow God. Six hundred and thirteen different ways, practices, and routines they had to be mindful of in order to be all God wanted them to be.

Now, ideally, these 613 laws would have created a society that mirrored Eden. In a failing present, these 613 laws would have ushered in a forgiving future. They were meant to return humanity to its most loving state. But rather than seeing these rules through the lens of a relationship with God the Father, Israel diminished them to just a list of rules that they had effectively abandoned by the time Micah came onto the scene.

So, in essence, Micah is operating out of this legalistic state that began with good intentions but has been twisted into a moralistic hamster wheel that never stops spinning. The people of Israel are trapped in a religious system rather than being free to live into a loving relationship.

God uses this moment to set the record straight. With the courtroom hushed, we are given God's closing argument.

The confusion of 613 rules has been whittled down to three distinct directives: Act justly. Love mercy. Walk humbly.

Three directives that are embodied seven centuries later in the person of Jesus of Nazareth. As Jesus himself said, "Do not think that I have come to abolish the Law or the Prophets; I have not come to abolish them but to fulfill them."[12]

And how are these laws fulfilled? Jesus sums it up: "'Love the Lord your God with all your heart and with all your soul and with all your mind.' This is the first and greatest commandment. And the second is like it: 'Love your neighbor as yourself.' All the Law and the Prophets hang on these two commandments."[13]

How do we counteract our failing present and usher in a forgiving future? Is there a way of being in the world that fights back against the injustices of the human condition? That helps us remember our forgiving God in a world rife with forgetfulness? The answer, of course, is yes.

God offers us the map. But here's the rub: if all that the great commandment comes down to is a bumper sticker on our car or a Bible verse to memorize, then it ceases to be the guiding truth of our lives and instead becomes a cliché with dangerous ideological power that lacks proximity.

Justice is the counteractive agent to this. Justice is the catalyst to bring about a forgiving future. Justice is what love looks like in action.

Jesus once warned against false prophets who can't bear good fruit.[14] My translation: "Hey! It's possible to appear like you're a follower of me, but your fruit—your actions—will exemplify whether you're truly my disciple."

Justice, mercy, and humility serve as the foundation of being a disciple of Jesus. When justice, mercy, and humility form the outer edges of our character, love permeates our being.

Cue Jesus' mic drop one-liner that we love to quote: "By this everyone will know that you are my disciples, if you love one another."[15] The apostle Paul put it this way: "Whoever loves others has fulfilled the law."[16]

God's court case against humanity is not an attempt to publicly crush us under the weight and shame of our sin. It's an invitation to remember. To remember that—despite our sin—God loves us. In fact, he loves us so much that he sent his one and only Son to die for us. Why? So that we could experience eternal life through him. While we are busy lodging complaints against him, he has already forgiven the weight of all our sin—for eternity. It's time for us to drop the stone. To forgive our forgiving Father.

Again—for anyone this seems familiar to—*don't miss this*. If we dumb down this concept to a cliché, we don't recognize its power. It's not less than a declaration of everlasting life, but it is *so* much more. If you believe within your heart and confess with your mouth that Jesus is Lord, you will be saved.[17] This is true. But Jesus is not simply offering us eternal life when we die; he's offering us eternal life *now*. John 10:10 says, "I have come that they may have life, and have it to the full." His offer of eternal life is an act of love.

Therefore, in *response* to this love, we seek to follow him. Not out of obligation but out of obedience. In doing so, we fulfill

Jesus' greatest command: to love the Lord our God with all of our heart, soul, mind, and strength and to love our neighbor as ourselves.

The only reasonable response to God's requirement is to act justly, love mercy, and walk humbly with him. To love because he first loved us. Mystery = solved. Case = closed.

Not only does God love us, forgive us, and offer us eternal life, but he invites us to partner with him in the restorative process of the coming new heaven and earth, as it was originally intended to be. Peter's vision offers us a prophetic picture of our future: "Since everything will be destroyed in this way, what kind of people ought you to be? You ought to live holy and godly lives as you look forward to the day of God and speed its coming. That day will bring about the destruction of the heavens by fire, and the elements will melt in the heat. But in keeping with his promise we are looking forward to a new heaven and a new earth, where righteousness dwells."[18]

Notice—in this present moment—Peter beckons humanity to live holy and godly lives in preparation for the forgiving, restorative future that is to come.

Justice, mercy, and humility are the ingredients for allowing *that* future into *this* present.

We must learn what it means to pursue biblical justice, mercy, and humility in order to secure a forgiving future. If justice is what love looks like in action, then the question becomes "How do we do it?" And how do we balance the tension between mercy and justice?

How do we participate with God—as coheirs and corulers in his Kingdom—by enacting justice, offering mercy, and taking up our cross to follow him?

1. ACT JUSTLY.

There is a name and a face behind justice. There is relational proximity to the other person. People cease to become political talking points and instead become humans to be loved, stories to be learned, and friendships to be grown.

Justice is concentrated on our neighbor. The person to the left or the right of us.

We must prayerfully discern: What is the holy discontent within us? Where do we sense God asking us to intervene? We can't fix everything, but each of us can do something.

No one demonstrated this more than Jesus. God in the flesh, he came and lived among us—the elites and the disenfranchised, the religious and the marginalized.

What's that line Jesus says in Matthew 16? "Whoever wants to be my disciple must deny themselves and take up their cross and follow me."[19]

Whoever. Now, last time I checked, whoever meant . . . *whoever*.

The invitation Jesus offers us is a life of comfort *in the midst of* suffering.

In his own words: "I have told you these things, so that in me you may have peace. In this world you will have trouble. But take heart! I have overcome the world."[20]

To be human is to struggle. To suffer. For things we've done, things done against us, or as a result of living in a fallen, broken world. This is the hold that sin has on the world. And within this reality, an ache is stirred that we all carry. A longing for something more, something better.

We long for justice and righteousness. For the world to be set right. As Jesus said, "Blessed are those who hunger and thirst for righteousness, for they will be filled."[21] We desire justice and hope for mercy but fail to recognize the forgiveness that has already been extended to us in the person of Jesus.

Biblical justice rests not in acts of charity—as great as those are—but rather, an end point where both the plentiful and hungry, Republican and Democrat, rich and poor, Black and white are seated at the table under the one heavenly Father.[22]

2. LOVE MERCY.

Jesus did not discriminate between the oppressed or the oppressor. He offered everlasting, eternal life to both the prostitute and the tax collector, the blind beggar and the rich young ruler. There was no "othering" in Jesus' posture toward people. He simply loved them. And out of that love—as the prophet Micah instructs us—he acted justly, loved mercy, and walked humbly with God.

Dr. Derwin L. Gray says this: *"Justice without Jesus is vengeance.* God's mercy is for the oppressor *and* the oppressed. Repentance of the oppressor, forgiveness from the oppressed, reconciliation of the enemies with human flourishing—these things are God's heart."[23]

To those of you who are struggling to extend mercy, I offer the words of the apostle James from James 2, which says, "Speak and act as those who are going to be judged by the law that gives freedom, because judgment without mercy will be shown to anyone who has not been merciful. Mercy triumphs over judgment."[24]

Mercy triumphs over judgment.

What offering mercy does is it opens our hearts to inviting Jesus to do what only he can do—we invite him in to inject in us the supernatural ability to offer undeserved mercy and in that, we are reminded of the undeserved mercy we ourselves are receiving at each present moment.

Mercy changes your *future* in Christ. It changes your testimony. It changes your identity. It changes your heart as you walk through life no longer as a victim but as a conqueror in Christ Jesus who has given you the strength to stand above those who tried to pull you down.

Mercy triumphs. Every time. In every situation.

3. WALK HUMBLY.

Humility is at the heart of forgiveness. We forgive because we were forgiven. We receive undeserved forgiveness from others because God gave each of us undeserved forgiveness himself. And God graciously allows us to repent and go another way.

When we fall short, consequences are often given to us for our corrective benefit. This is the side of God that we do not want to talk about. A God of grace and mercy seems too loving to bring about any sort of judgment on anyone, right? But "God cannot be mocked" and "[he] cannot tolerate wrongdoing."[25] So, like a good parent—he uses consequences to correct and discipline his children, not simply to punish them but to redirect them into becoming the inheritors of his Kingdom he has promised we will be.

The ability to choose between right and wrong afforded to us by God is the essence of how much he loves us. He does not force us into obedience or blind allegiance. Neither does he passively observe. Instead, he inserts himself directly into the human story in a demonstration of humility: "He made himself nothing by taking the very nature of a servant, being made in human likeness. And being found in appearance as a man, he humbled himself by becoming obedient to death—even death on a cross!"[26]

In our journey of forgiveness, there will come a time when temptation to return to our old ways surfaces. It's in those moments that we must regularly recommit to the new way of life that we have chosen and follow the example of humility that has been set for us. Daily, we surrender our pride, we pick up our cross, and we follow Jesus. This can't be done alone.

We confess our sins to God and in return, God forgives us and mercifully cleanses us to return to right relationship with him. This is a beautiful paradigm of our relationship to God.

Jesus invites us to a journey: to increase in suffering love. Learning to love God with all our heart, soul, mind, and strength and to love our neighbor as ourselves. Acting justly, loving mercy, and walking humbly with him. Even when it costs us, even when names are called, even when exclusion happens, even when misunderstandings take place. Even if humiliation, shame, or persecution arises, we must not back down. For through life's suffering, we find Jesus.

As we grow in suffering love, not only do we find Jesus, but we find those whom Jesus loved as well. The outcast and the ostracized, the tyrant and the timid, the wealthy yet empty and the weeping yet full. Costly love transforms us to look more and more like the Wounded Healer himself—our forgiving Savior.

Justice—on this side of heaven—is not always enacted properly. We should grieve this and seek to rectify unjust situations whenever we can. But injustice is not an excuse for unforgiveness. Unforgiveness, in the face of injustice, does more damage to our soul than anything else possibly could.

———

In 1994, 80 percent of Rwandans were attending church the Sunday before a civil war broke out. A genocide of nearly a million people ensued over the next hundred days.[27] A display of violence, hatred, and anger so devastating that it sent shock waves throughout the world.

In 2014, twenty years after these horrific events ensued, a photographer named Pieter Hugo from the *New York Times* traveled to southern Rwanda to capture the most unlikely, yet profoundly biblical portraits.

The men and women who agreed to be photographed are a part of an ongoing effort of national reconciliation being shepherded by the nonprofit AMI (Association Modeste et Innocent). The AMI's program includes intensive counseling over the course of many months, culminating in a formal request of forgiveness by the perpetrator.

The portraits are truly stunning.

They show the (understood) shame many of the perpetrators carried. These were mostly neighbors who became pawns in the harshest of political, ethnic, and power divides. But the perpetrators also took responsibility for their actions. There was no denying, whitewashing, or diminishing the pain, hurt, and destruction. Instead, there was an acceptance of what was and an invitation of what could be.

What's more striking are the emotions many of the victims and survivors shared as they forgave those who had—in many cases—brutally murdered loved ones, burned homes, and stolen everything of value. Feelings of peace, acceptance, and clarity were prevalent.

Here's how one survivor of the Rwandan genocide, Karorero, put it: "Sometimes justice does not give someone a satisfactory answer—[legal] cases are subject to corruption. But when it comes to forgiveness willingly granted, one is satisfied once and for all. When someone is full of anger, he can lose his mind. But when I granted forgiveness, I felt my mind at rest."[28]

We have much to learn from our Rwandan brothers and sisters. The United States is witnessing division, hostility, and polarization—many historians agree—not seen since the Civil War.[29]

Over the last forty years, social psychologist James Averill has been tracking the effects of anger in America. From his initial study in 1977 until the mid-2010s, Averill noted how anger permeated our nation. In 2016, as the political divide in the US began to widen and polarization became increasingly prevalent, Averill began to notice a shift.

Anger, Averill noted, would be the fuel to drive the American people toward particular political agendas. Outrage—serving as a compelling, persuasive emotion—signaled a shift in American civility and union. The journalist Charles Duhigg, in his analysis on Averill's study, wrote,

> Recently, however, the tenor of our anger has shifted. It has become less episodic and more persistent, a constant drumbeat in our lives. It is directed less often at people we

know and more often at distant groups that are easy to demonize. These far-off targets may or may not have earned our ire; either way, they're apt to be less invested in resolving our differences. . . . Without the release of catharsis, our anger has built within us, exerting an unwanted pressure that can have a dark consequence: the desire not merely to be heard, but to hurt those we believe have wronged us.[30]

Our inability to deal with our anger is costing us dearly.

As Pastor Jon Tyson commented, "The progress in our world today has come with unintended consequences." He goes on to say, "So many men have been wounded by the wars of the modern world. Political wars, relational wars, vocational wars, family wars. So many men walk around with gaping wounds in their hearts."[31]

Think about it: these wounds are expressing themselves through increasing rates of fatherlessness and confusion around masculinity, identity, value, and worth. The anger many men experience is a prime example of the cost of being malformed in the ways of the world. We have chosen to settle for surface-level reactions rather than deep transformation, and it has left us feeling stuck between ambition and ambivalence. Not so much anxious but aimless. In a word, we're *languishing*. Unsure of how to move forward with intention and drive.

As a culture, we seem to be moving the opposite direction of a forgiving future. If we're not careful, we may end up repeating the same mistakes of history's past. We must learn what it means to pursue biblical justice in order to secure a forgiving future.

Forgiving is a scary but necessary proposition. In offering forgiveness, we do not admit defeat. We do not let "the enemy" (be it another human or Satan himself) win. In fact, forgiveness helps us overcome. In forgiving, we have a chance for our heart to heal. Because to live is to forgive. The opposite of forgiveness is resentment. And to press into resentment is to die a slow soul death. As someone I dearly love once said, "Forgiveness prevents forfeiting your future by not living in your past."[32] When we forgive, the enemy doesn't win. Christ wins. Christ—and his reconciling image—is on display for all the world to see through you.

As followers of Jesus, reconciliation must always be our ultimate desire. A forgiving future must be our aim. Reconciliation is central to our story because it is the crux of God's story. He is a forgiving God. Reconciliation is at the very core of the gospel—the Good News—of Jesus. It is what distinguishes us—in part—as followers of Jesus. We are to be Christ's "ambassadors" of his reconciliation to the world.[33]

Envision a future where reconciliation is normalized. Where justice, mercy, and humility are anchors to a countercultural community. Where consequences and boundaries exist but love permeates as the signifying exclamation point on our lives. God will one day return to reclaim and reconcile all of creation. What was once deemed the greatest failure imaginable (Christ's death) led to the greatest victory (the Resurrection) and will return as the most triumphant redemption of all time.

When it's our turn to step onto the stand, what will our defense be? We've already been proclaimed guilty . . . But wait. Jesus steps up to take our place. God is finding us—not guilty. Whatever sins you've been holding on to, whatever hurt you've experienced, it's already forgiven and made right. Our failing present is not the end of the story. Remember? God has not forgotten you.

Our forgiven future is already secure.

12

FORGIVENESS IS FOR EVERYONE (YES, EVERYONE)

"TRULY I TELL YOU, TODAY YOU WILL BE with me in paradise."[1]

I've always struggled with this statement from Jesus. To set the scene, Jesus is hanging on a cross between two criminals. The people below are mocking Jesus ad nauseam: "He saved others; let him save himself if he is God's Messiah, the Chosen One." The Roman soldiers are mocking him too. And then one of the criminals chimes in, "Aren't you the Messiah? Save yourself and us!"[2]

Then the other criminal responds. "'Don't you fear God,' he [says], 'since you are under the same sentence? We are punished justly, for we are getting what our deeds deserve. But this man has done nothing wrong.'"[3]

This criminal then audaciously asks Jesus to remember him when Jesus enters the Kingdom of Heaven.[4] And Jesus' answer? "Truly I tell you, today you will be with me in paradise."[5]

Seriously?

Just like that?

So, is this man's whole life of criminal activity negated? Wiped out? Like it didn't happen?

These are the thoughts—at my worst—that run through my head. *That it isn't fair.*

Jesus' forgiveness certainly isn't fair objectively speaking. But is forgiveness actually equal? And this brings up a host of larger questions: Who deserves forgiveness? Who can receive forgiveness? Who should I forgive?

The answer to these questions is either infuriating or inspiring, depending on your viewpoint. My hope is that through examining forgiveness we can come to understand how Jesus' Good News is the only possible hope we have for the life to come and for achieving any peace in our present life.

There's a question that—in our journey to launch into and engage as authentic followers of Jesus in this world—we have to answer: "Who should I forgive?"

Him? Her? Does someone like *that* deserve forgiveness? On the surface, our immediate rational reaction would be "absolutely not."

But the way of Jesus leads to a curious life. As we ask questions, compassion, mercy, and empathy grow within our hearts, leading us to do extraordinary things. Forgiveness being one of them.

How? In a world that's full of pain, hurt, and darkness, how could anyone who has ever hurt, betrayed, lied to, or abused us deserve our forgiveness?

It's an unfair question with an unfair answer that is the most hope-filled outcome possible.

After Jesus' death and resurrection, he appears before his disciples and announces his presence with a single sentence: "Peace be with you!"[6] He repeats this phrase, then follows up with a curious imperative: "Receive the Holy Spirit. If you forgive anyone's sins, their sins are forgiven; if you do not forgive them, they are not forgiven."[7] Now, these two lines may seem to be disconnected, but they are intimately intertwined. We'll return to this soon.

To recap, three days earlier, Jesus was abandoned, deserted, betrayed, and forgotten by these (now eleven) men. These disciples whom he had invested the last three years of his life into, built intimate relationships with, trusted, confided in, and developed as apprentices—these were the men that he was interacting with for the first time since all of that took place. Three years of investment had been seemingly crushed in three days.

Can you imagine?

Can you imagine pouring everything into a person or relationship just for them to abandon, betray, or backstab you? Most of us probably can, right? Who comes to mind?

It's likely that you see yourself in Jesus' story.

I know what that's like.

The pain of rejection, of division. The embarrassment of having believed that someone was who we thought they were.

So Jesus, with all of that relational baggage and history in tow, arrives on the scene for the first time post-Resurrection with an announcement: Peace. Be. With. You.

What?! Peace be with you? How about "You imbeciles. You idiots. You cowards! You abandoned me. I gave you so many chances and you blew it! How could you be so stupid, so ignorant, so wrong?"

Peace be with you.

What *is* this?

This is forgiveness at its finest, my friend.

The disciples deserved a word of rebuke, of blame, of shame. Instead, they were offered a word of peace. And not "peace" in the kumbaya, let's-all-get-along sense. But in the *shalom* sense.[8] Broken parts made whole. Relational restoration. It is this peace that Jesus puts on full display. Reconciling shalom. God's forgiveness.

It's fascinating that Jesus follows up this announcement of peace by saying, "If you forgive anyone's sins, their sins are forgiven; if you do not forgive them, they are not forgiven."[9] The result of receiving the Holy Spirit was the ability to announce the forgiveness of the Cross. This is the same charge now given to the church.

Forgiveness becomes a message to either accept or reject. Jesus has empowered and authorized us—as his followers—to declare the Good News of his forgiveness. It is not ours to withhold or rescind. He alone is the judge of the world. We are the messenger; he is the message.

Jesus' entrance and greeting are unthinkable, unless you understand who Jesus is. The message "peace be with you" is Good News for all who hear it. It echoes the gospel that Jesus has been preaching all along: a gospel of repentance, forgiveness, reconciliation, and restoration.

And this Good News? It's for everyone.

Yes, *everyone*.

> For if you forgive other people when they sin against you, your heavenly Father will also forgive you. But *if you do not* forgive others their sins, your Father will *not* forgive your sins.[10]

> Do not judge, and you will not be judged. Do not condemn, and you will not be condemned. Forgive, and you will be forgiven.[11]

> And when you stand praying, if you hold anything against anyone, forgive them, so that your Father in heaven may forgive you your sins.[12]
>
> So watch yourselves. "If your brother or sister sins against you, rebuke them; and if they repent, forgive them. Even if they sin against you seven times in a day and seven times come back to you saying 'I repent,' you *must* forgive them."[13]

This Good News is for everyone; no ifs, ands, or buts about it.

"Well, that's not fair!"

"You don't understand what was done to me."

"You don't know what happened."

I don't disagree with you. However, Jesus does: "If you do not forgive others their sins, your Father will not forgive your sins."[14]

This is one of the most explicit statements on forgiveness that Jesus offers throughout all the Gospels, and it is *scandalous*. To those of you coming to these pages wounded, hurt, in pain, bitter, or resentful, I want you to know that I see you. I wish there was a way to dismiss, deny, or explain away this teaching. It certainly would justify the internal bitterness and strife we hold on to, wouldn't it?

As I mentioned, I'm in the boat with you here. "Truly I tell you, today you will be with me in paradise."[15] *Him? Really, Jesus? This man is a crook. He's on a cross for a reason. He deserves this punishment. I don't deserve that. I haven't done anything that bad. I'm not like him.* These are a few of the honest thoughts that run through my head when I read about this interaction.

But Jesus is clear: unforgiveness leads to unforgiveness. There's truly only one way forward. The spiritual writer Henri Nouwen said it this way: "By not forgiving, I chain myself to a desire to get even, thereby losing my freedom. A forgiven person forgives. This is what we proclaim when we pray 'and forgive us our trespasses as we forgive those who have trespassed against us.' This lifelong struggle lies at the heart of the Christian life."[16]

So, if we can't explain away the need to forgive, then what can we do? Well, we can do our best to work through Jesus' teaching to get clarity on what he's not saying, what he is saying, and what that means for us.

So first, here's what Jesus is not saying forgiveness is:

EXCUSING[17]

Forgiveness is not excusing or minimizing the injustice that has been done. Your pain and hurt are valid. Excusing an offense simply kicks the proverbial can down the road. That hurt and pain—real as it is—will continue to gnaw at you as you find ways to justify and dismiss what has occurred. At some point, the wrong must be acknowledged, forgiveness extended, and reconciliation pursued.

DENYING

Forgiveness is not pretending that an offense didn't happen. This is where the harmful adage "forgive and forget" comes into play. That expression is often used to mean "forget about what happened and move on." That's not forgiveness; that's an unhealthy form of denial that lets the offender off the hook. True repentance often requires costly repairs on the part of the offender.

To come back to the debt analogy, this would be like looking at a pile of cash in a room that someone owes you and hearing them say, "That doesn't exist. That's not there. That didn't happen." It's factually untrue, but the longer you hear it, the easier it becomes to believe. Forgiveness, however, at its essence requires a cost. It costs the perpetrator an unbelievable amount of humility to repent and ask for forgiveness, and it requires the offended to extend an unreasonable amount of humility to cancel the very real relational debt that's present in the room.

HOLDING ON TO AN OFFENSE

On the other end of the spectrum, some might say, "I'll forgive, but I'll never forget." How do you forgive what seems to be unforgettable?

The two words "never forget" probably jolt to mind the 9/11 terrorist attack of 2001. Our country rallied around the mantra "never forget."

For most, this was a phrase dedicated to pay homage to the victims and a promise to never forget the tragedy that unfolded that day.

For others, it became a rallying cry for revenge against the parties responsible for the attack.[18]

But to "never forget" in the case of forgiveness is an oxymoron. Instead of cancelling the debt, when we hold on to hurt, it creates an invisible, perpetual relational schism until the offended decides the debt has been paid—subjectively speaking. When we refuse to move on from an offense, we hold the offender in a prison of our own making—and we hold ourselves there too. When we remain stuck in this place, we fail to remember that, in his grace, God doesn't hold on to our own sins.

Forgiveness lies not with remembering or forgetting but with removing. "For as high as the heavens are above the earth, so great is his love for those who fear him; as far as the east is from the west, so far has he *removed* our transgressions from us."[19]

SUSPENDING JUDGMENT

Often we will brush aside what we deem to be "smaller offenses" subjectively speaking. So if someone makes a rude comment in passing at a dinner table and apologizes, we may reluctantly offer a word of forgiveness, but internally, we're thinking, *But if you ever . . .* That is not forgiveness; that is suspending judgment. We are secretly holding on to the offense, waiting for an opportune time to unload all past grievances onto the other person.

This is—classically—what we call resentment. Resentment may feel good in the short term, as it allows us to feel superior to the person we're holding an offense over. We also tend to write a bit of revisionist history. The further away we get from the offense, while clinging to resentment, the more we become emblazoned as the "decent" person who was attacked rather than a sinner in solidarity with the human condition that befits us all. But in the long term, resentment is a bitter pill that intoxicates our soul with contempt for the person who has wronged us. Resentment seems to justify our feelings while simultaneously robbing us of gratitude.

We must learn to let go of resentment, judgment, and bitterness so that we may receive the gratitude, mercy, and love that is offered to us when true forgiveness is experienced.

OFFERING CONDITIONAL FORGIVENESS

Forgiveness that is held over someone is no longer forgiveness—it is a weaponization of the good, free, undeserved gift of mercy that's first been given to us. Forgiveness with conditions is not true, biblical forgiveness. Forgiveness refers to a debt cancellation, not a debt deference, consolidation, or redefinition. The debt is effectively no more. Attaching strings to our forgiveness creates an unequal dynamic in the relationship, putting the forgiver in a position of power or control and the person in need of forgiveness in the position of fear or shame.

ABANDONING JUSTICE

This is where many get caught up.

"Aren't I just letting them off the hook?"

Not exactly.

Forgiveness is not the absence of justice. Justice upholds an expectation that when someone has wronged someone else (and God), the offense requires confession of sin to God and to the person who was wronged. Justice also requires accepting the consequences as commanded by God or societal law. Even if the wrong was accidental or unintentional, there are ramifications for the decisions we make. Justice and righteousness are the engine of loving reconciliation.[20]

Justice is necessary for God's sake, for the victim's sake, and for the wrongdoer's sake.[21]

Author and pastor Timothy Keller writes, "People tend to either seek personal revenge in the belief that that *is* justice or not seek any justice at all. One is vindictiveness and the other cowardice."[22] In other words, true forgiveness requires justice. But justice without Jesus becomes retaliation. We must seek what *is* fair and good, not what our emotions tell us is fair or feels good.

IMMEDIATE TRUST

There's a tendency in Christian thought to confuse the process of reconciliation with the act of forgiveness. This is a tragic mistake. Not only is it unhealthy, but often it can be harmful—for instance, citing Matthew 18:15-20 should not be an excuse for maintaining an abusive relationship.[23]

Until a person has repented, desires reconciliation, and demonstrates true, actionable progress toward said reconciliation, they shouldn't be entrusted with restored relationship. This is not only accountability for the perpetrator, but also protection for the wronged.

For those in spiritual authority (i.e., as a pastor, elder, deacon, small group leader, etc.), we are entrusted with stewarding these situations with great care and attentiveness. Encouraging premature reconciliation could actually be ammo for someone caught in sin to continue sinning (why would they quit if there are no consequences?).

Please don't mishear me; we should ever be working toward reconciliation (which we'll get to). That is our mandate as followers of Jesus seeking to see heaven on earth. However, the speed at which that reconciliation takes place and whether relational proximity is possible should be thought through with prudence, wisdom, and care.

My dad, after his infamous affair, was removed from public ministry for over four years, and even when he was restored, it was not to a lead pastor position for ten years total. (Incidentally, ten years is what the professor and therapist Chuck DeGroat recommends regarding pastoral restoration after a moral failing.[24]) This should not be seen as a hard-and-fast rule, but as a general principle that the duration and intensity of the process should match the weight of the offense.

If those approaches are what Jesus is *not* saying forgiveness is, then what are the qualities of forgiveness? Well, I see it as a decision that is part of an ongoing process. In fact, there are three facets to the decisive act of forgiveness.

1. FORGIVENESS IS A *RESPONSIVE* DECISION.

Forgiveness is first and foremost a reality that those of us who follow Jesus are enveloped in. The mandate to forgive is because "the Lord [has forgiven] you."[25] It is in response to Jesus' lavish, undeserving mercy that we are able to offer mercy to others.

In response to Jesus' forgiveness, we act. The late pastor Charles Stanley writes, "*Forgiveness* is *the act* of setting someone free from an obligation to you that is a result of a wrong done against you."[26] Author Lysa Terkeurst notes, "Forgiveness isn't an act of my *determination*. Forgiveness is only made possible by my *cooperation*."[27]

Do you see it? They're hinting at the same thing. Forgiveness is a *choice*. But it's not merely an act of the will; it's an act of response. Who *really* wants to forgive someone who has wronged or hurt them? I didn't think so. Instead, we respond to the grace that was first extended to us on the cross.

Forgiveness, then, is the intentional decision to graciously extend what I have undeservedly received—the cancellation of my sinful debt that has incurred (either in an instant or over time).

A few weeks ago, a friend sent a text to Rylei and me that (unintentionally) came across hurtful. Worse, it was sent as my head hit the pillow. I wouldn't have seen it until the next day (when I would have been in a far better state of mind), but Rylei happened to still be on her phone (tsk, tsk . . .).

"Did you read this?"

"Read what?" I asked, trying to pretend like I was asleep even though I'd just turned out my light.

Of course, I got up, read the text, and immediately felt anxiety and anger coursing through my veins. Had I replied in the moment, it would have been a reactive decision based on my emotions.

Forgiveness requires a responsive decision. So we waited until the following day, called our friend, and were able to hash out how the tone of the text made us feel. Of course, our friend profusely apologized, and out of that place, we were able to offer forgiveness and reconcile. After taking time to respond, we moved into the next step in the process: creating an opportunity to restore relationship.

2. FORGIVENESS IS A *RELATIONAL* DECISION.

Forgiveness is—at its best—a starting point. Whenever it is within our control and healthy to pursue, forgiveness acts as a vehicle on a journey of reconciliation. A social fabric has been torn, which needs mending. When we forgive, we reconcile—or heal—what has been hurt. We restore what has been broken. This creates a social dynamic that is prophetic in nature, pointing people around us to a future reality where sinner, saint, and skeptic alike will commune at the table together. Forgiveness and the pursuit of reconciliation serves as a foretaste of the new heaven and earth to come. Because we are in relationship with a forgiving God, we are empowered to pursue grace and reconciliation in relation to our neighbor.

Forgiveness, as much as it depends on us, can't end with us. Forgiving others is healing and transformative for *my* heart. But reconciling is healing and transformative for *our* hearts.

When I position my feelings, wants, needs, and desires as ultimate, the relational aspect of forgiveness gets lost at best or is outright rejected at worst. When instead I focus on extending grace to the other person, compassion opens the door to understanding, leading to the renewed relationship.

Throughout this writing process, I've been convicted that there are people in my life whom I've forgiven but not reconciled with.

As best I can, where appropriate, I've tried to reach out to these people and name that. I'm not ultimately in control of reconciliation taking place, but I am always in control of initiating the process should I feel prompted to.

As followers of Jesus, understanding the relational component of forgiveness in the form of reconciliation offers us a countercultural, heavenly vision of restoration. What was once broken is made whole and redeemed.

3. FORGIVENESS IS A *REQUIRED* DECISION.

This is potentially the most difficult aspect of forgiveness to swallow. However, Jesus is explicit in the Scriptures: "For if you forgive other people when they sin against you, your heavenly Father will also forgive you. But if you do not forgive others their sins, your Father will not forgive your sins."[28]

There's no explaining away or sidestepping this imperative from Jesus. There is a reciprocal nature to forgiveness. Forgiveness extended, forgiveness received. Forgiveness withheld, forgiveness rejected.

That being said, we must continue to distinguish forgiveness from excuse. Forgiveness is a voluntary form of suffering. We can't deny or minimize the cost, and we can't deny or minimize the consequences. Through forgiveness, both realities can exist.

I recently wrote a letter to someone who wounded me almost ten years ago. In the letter, I did my best to graciously offer forgiveness without excusing the poor choices that had led to our decade of separation. I've needed that time to heal, but over the last few years, I've sensed God pushing me to where I knew I would inevitably end up — in a position to extend forgiveness. There is no relationship in my life that I've felt okay withholding forgiveness in. No matter how badly someone has wounded me, I consistently sense the imperative to work toward forgiving them. This journey is often to my benefit. I've seen time and time again God use for good what Satan meant for evil. Forgiveness has convinced me to try again even when I don't feel like it. Resentment has tempted me to quit altogether. No matter what the circumstances are, I lose when I choose resentment.

Jesus commands us to forgive for our *good*. Just because it doesn't feel good doesn't mean it isn't good. And in the end, we experience a depth of freedom through forgiveness that is unexplainable until it is authentically practiced.

This is the way of the Cross. This is the way of Jesus. Costly grace on the part of our Savior with an invitation to practice costly grace toward our neighbor.

So, what does this mean for us?

Let's return to Jesus and the Cross. "When they came to the place called the Skull, they crucified [Jesus] there, along with the criminals—one on his right, the other on his left. Jesus said, 'Father, forgive them, for they do not know what they are doing.'"[29]

At this, people all around him start mocking Jesus. A sign is hung above his head that reads, "THIS IS THE KING OF THE JEWS" as if to make it painfully obvious that this man is a fraud.

The criminal to his right says, "Are you serious? You call yourself the savior? If you're the savior, then *save us! Save yourself!*" But the other criminal rebukes him. He says, "How dare you talk to this man like that. You and I are up here because we deserve it. This guy, this Jesus, he's done *nothing* wrong, and yet here he hangs."

Then he turns to Jesus and says, "Jesus, if you're willing, forgive me. I'm a sinful man, and I've done some bad things in my life. Remember me when you come into your Kingdom."[30] And here's Jesus' stunning response: "Truly I tell you, today you will be with me in paradise."[31]

Who is forgiveness for? According to Jesus, it's for

> The lowest of the low.
>
> The betrayers.
>
> The liars.
>
> The insulters.

My friends, it's for you and me. How can that be?

First John 4:19 about sums it up: "We love because he first loved us." We *forgive* because he first *forgave* us. Forgiveness is for everyone. Yes, everyone. The sooner that we're able to grasp that truth, the less time will we spend under the rule and reign of bitterness and resentment that chokes the life out of us.

There is a way—a better way—forward. And that way offers you freedom that can only be experienced by making an intentional decision—a decision that is responsive, relational, and required—to forgive. This is—of course—easier said than done, but it is possible.

A week after first appearing to his disciples, Jesus appears to them *again* with the same phrase: "Peace be with you!" This verse gives us some interesting insight into their present state. Here it is in full: "A week later his disciples were in the house again, and Thomas was with them. *Though the doors were locked*, Jesus came and stood among them and said, 'Peace be with you!'"[32]

A week later. The disciples have seen Jesus with their own eyes. They know he's alive. They know he is who he says he is. And yet . . . "the doors were locked."

Jesus came, once again, stood among them, and said, "Peace be with you!"

My friend, is this not mind-blowing to you? Because it is to me. Jesus enters this house not once but *twice*. A house full of deserters and deniers. A house full of backstabbers and friends who ran away when things got hard.

Jesus enters that house a week later, finding his apprentices in the same fetal position as before—despite their contact and interaction with the resurrected Jesus—and he leads with "peace be with you."

Healing words. Forgiving words. Redemption and restoration in one fell swoop.

Are we surprised? We shouldn't be. This is who Jesus is! And it's who he calls us to be as well.

Forgiveness is not easy. It's not natural. It's not desirable—unless we're the ones asking for it. It's not expected—at a cultural level. But it is demanded by a God who first forgave us. Who demonstrated forgiveness over and over . . . and over again.

Our invitation is to pray for "[God to] supply the feeling" and then be obedient to the required action—to forgive.[33] As we do, coldness turns to warmth, distance turns to proximity, strife turns to compassion, and fractures turn to healing.

Who is forgiveness for? It's for the criminal on the cross. It's for the disciples who abandoned, betrayed, and denied Jesus as Lord repeatedly. It's for you and me.

As the apostle John writes, "For God so loved the world that he gave his one and only Son, that whoever believes in him shall not perish but have eternal life."[34]

Whoever? Whoever.

The net is cast as far as the eye can see. And praise God, that net includes you and me.

13

THREE STRIKES, YOU'RE FORGIVEN

WE INTUITIVELY UNDERSTAND . . . three strikes, you're out. Three failures seem to be the built-in breaking point for most of us. As the famous adage goes, "Fool me once, shame on you. Fool me twice, shame on me . . ." Notice, there's not a "fool me three times . . ."

Jewish rabbinical tradition in ancient Israel only required that forgiveness be extended three times. Were three failures the breaking point even for Jesus? He seems to answer this question in Mark 14.

Jesus and his disciples are sharing a meal together on the eve of his crucifixion, burial, and resurrection. Jesus clearly explains what is going to happen, but the disciples don't seem to get it.

Finally, Jesus stops mincing words. "'You will all fall away,' Jesus [tells] them, 'for it is written: "I will strike the shepherd, and the sheep will be scattered." But after I have risen, I will go ahead of you into Galilee.'"[1]

This is an ominous line, isn't it? A statement many of us would take offense to if we were the disciples, right? Well, lo and behold, one disciple in particular takes great exception: "Peter declared, 'Even if all fall away, I will not.' 'Truly I tell you,' Jesus answered, 'today—yes, tonight—before the rooster crows twice you yourself will disown me *three* times.' But Peter insisted emphatically, 'Even if I have to die with you, I will never disown you.' And all the others said the same."[2]

It's easy to make grand claims when there are low stakes. But when the lights turn on and the pressure rises, the false self is burned away and what is left is our true self, who we really are. Jesus was hinting at the fact that Peter was not as loyal, brave, or devoted as he thought he was.

This interaction has haunted me. When the stakes are raised, when things that I frivolously care about—my ego, reputation, persona, public approval, popularity—are on the line, will I capitulate to the crowd or to the Cross?

Jesus goes one way, and he hints that Peter is going to go another . . .

Mark then cuts to another scene of Jesus with his disciples in the garden of Gethsemane. Jesus instructs them to "sit here while I pray."[3] He takes Peter, James, and John with him and gives them specific instructions to keep watch.

While Jesus is wrestling his own fear to the ground, Peter, James, and John fail their one assignment. When Jesus returns, they're fast asleep.

Notice who Jesus singles out: "'Simon,' he said to Peter, 'are you asleep? Couldn't you keep watch for one hour? Watch and pray so that you will not fall into temptation. The spirit is willing, but the flesh is weak.'"[4]

It's almost as if he's saying, "Peter, didn't you just say that you wouldn't abandon me? I gave you a simple instruction to keep watch for an hour and you fell asleep. I'm giving you the opportunity to go a different way. Pray. Stay alert. Because I know you want to follow me, but you're struggling with temptation and that will lead you where you swore you wouldn't go."

When I have most strongly battled temptation in my life, it has often been at night, when my body is weak, my mind tired, and my energy low. The disciples were in the same situation. Jesus instructs Peter to press into prayer as a means to overcome the temptation he is facing. If only Peter had listened . . .

Jesus goes back to pray and returns to find them sleeping *again*. Their embarrassment leaves them without words.[5] Jesus goes back to pray a *third* time and returns a *third* time and finally says, "*Enough*."[6] At this point, Jesus' betrayers have come. Time's up. Three failures, they're out.

Surely, at this point, Peter's willingness to recommit to Jesus is even stronger than before? I mean, Jesus called out that Peter would disown him, and when they go to the garden, Peter's actions seem to prove Jesus right. Maybe now Peter will find the courage to follow through on his pledge?

Not quite.

Although Peter does stay near Jesus when all the other disciples desert him, a servant girl of the high priest ends up raising the stakes and revealing who Peter really is. She identifies him as one of Jesus' followers. His response? "I don't know or understand what you're talking about."[7]

But the servant girl doesn't let it go. "He's one of them!"[8] Again, Peter denies it. A third time, others standing nearby say, "Surely you are one of them, for you are a Galilean."[9] At this, Peter swears that he "[doesn't] know [the] man."[10]

Immediately the rooster crows a second time. Peter remembers Jesus' words—*before the rooster crows twice you yourself will disown me three times*—and he breaks down and weeps.[11] Three denials . . . Peter's out.

This is the last time we hear from Peter in the Gospel of Mark. It's an ominous, disturbing end. A prophecy fulfilled. Peter the denier. Peter the liar. Peter the abandoner.

Taken at face value, this is the defining moment of Peter's life. The proverbial period at the end of the sentence. How could it not be? Peter had three chances. And you know what the rule of the day was? Three failures, you're out.

The next day, Jesus hung on a cross, and for three hours, darkness came over all the land.[12] It seemed like the tale of three was winning in the end. Perhaps failure was final after all.

Except that's not the end of the story. Three days later, Jesus would come to redefine and reshape our imagination around three chances. Apparently, the Kingdom of Heaven is bigger than our preconceived notions about forgiveness and failure.

In Matthew 5, Jesus teaches, "Therefore, if you are offering your gift at the altar and there remember that your brother or sister has something against you, leave your gift there in front of the altar. First go and be reconciled to them; then come and offer your gift."[13] He is saying, "Look, if you're going to worship me, if you're going to follow me, then you must learn to *forgive*."

Not forget. Not turn a blind eye. Not excuse. *Forgive.*

Jesus has credibility to say these words. This is a man who was abused, beaten, spit on, physically attacked, publicly shamed, relationally abandoned, and deeply hurt. And yet, to those very people, Jesus says, "Father, forgive them, for they do not know what they are doing."[14]

Your hurt is real. So was Jesus'. But the Scriptures have insight that we would be wise to accept. "Get rid of all bitterness, rage and anger, brawling and slander, along with every form of malice. Be kind and compassionate to one another, forgiving each other, just as in Christ God forgave you."[15]

There is a thread here that can be traced through the New Testament. Unforgiveness only prolongs and spreads hurt. At some point, we must be willing to do the work of repair—for no one's sake more than our own.

Think about how radical Jesus' teachings are. In a cultural moment that is increasingly polarized, divisive, and extreme, the King of kings says to "love your enemies and pray for those who persecute you."[16] This is countercultural to the world around us. It's opposed to our sinful, fallen nature.

Forgiveness rarely feels good. Why? Because it costs something. In fact, it costs a lot. To forgive costs us greatly.

My point is this: if we wait to forgive until we are in a better emotional state, we could be waiting forever. Forgiveness transcends human brokenness because forgiveness transcends human reasoning and logic. It is fundamentally unfair. And yet, it is radically fulfilling.

I'm struck by how often Jesus finishes a teaching on forgiveness with the caveat "so that your Father in heaven may forgive you your sins."[17] We *receive* forgiveness when we *extend* forgiveness.

Failing to forgive past offenses hurts no one more than ourselves. And Jesus knows this. He understands how much *more* it matters for us to start the process of healing even if we didn't start the process that led to hurt. He knows that forgiveness may not change the other person's heart, motives, or future direction. However, true, authentic forgiveness always changes our heart, motives, and future direction. And it is out of this posture that we discover the scandal of grace to its fullest extent.

As I reflect on my life so far, I see the fruit of forgiveness in all areas of my complex familial history.

October 16—the date my dad left—comes and goes, and every year my parents commemorate that awful day from 2005 with a private dinner. As the years have passed, people have routinely asked me, "How in the world did you forgive your dad?" I usually responded with some awkward platitude.

However, the longer that it's been since that day and the more that I've reflected, the more I've realized that my journey of forgiving my dad has not been as linear as I'd like it to be.

The crucible of hours of intensive counseling, months of conversation, and years of rebuilding trust forged my forgiveness. I initially forgave my dad after he moved back in and my parents renewed their wedding vows. That was the moment when I first made the definitive decision to give my dad another chance. He once again had my love, but he did not quite have my respect, trust, loyalty, or support . . . yet. That came with time. Over time, I saw a broken man become a changed man. And that changed man is the dad I love today.

Failure isn't final, but forgiveness also isn't easy.

There have been days, weeks, months, and even years when the hurt of what could've been rises to the surface of my soul. At age ten, I had everything taken away from me, without a say. It was unfair. It was frustrating. And it was painful. But I also had many beautiful experiences, built wonderful relationships, and learned incredible things in the aftermath of my dad's biggest failure. I wouldn't trade what I've received as a result of what I lost. What Satan meant for evil, God used for good![18]

As an eighteen-year-old, watching my godfather make similar choices to leave a church and his family was tremendously painful. And yet, over time, I have forgiven him for walking out of my life. Part of this process meant writing him an email communicating this decision and saying these words: "I forgive you." I'm immensely grateful for the ways he has shaped and formed me. I have intentionally kept over one hundred of his sermon outlines, which I still treasure. I appreciate the profound influence he's had on my life. And I've come to appreciate how his mistakes have directly informed how I do and do *not* want to pastor. We must wisely discern how our past will influence our present.

The pain of my family of origin's hidden past arises every year around the holidays. We gather sparsely and celebrate momentous occasions here and there on both sides. But even as I've reflected on that reality, I've come to deeply appreciate all the wonderful ways my grandparents—blood and adopted—have formed and shaped me. Both sides of our extended family have made sacrifices for one another. I can name how individuals have come through when I've needed them most. It's not perfect, and there's certainly still hurt and pain to wade through, but at the end of the day, I've realized this: gratitude has become the pervasive characteristic of my life journey.

Mercy wins.

Forgiveness wins.

Why?

Because through the ups and downs, the good and bad, the beautiful and broken moments, I've experienced a God who forgives me without condition.

How in the world could you forgive _____? You fill in the blank.

My honest answer? How could we not?

Each and every day, I find myself messing up, falling short, and missing the mark. If you were able to live inside my head for a day (a horrible hypothetical), you would throw this book into a fire and probably try to throw me in with it. I am a wretched sinner, saved by grace. So are my dad, my godfather, and my grandpas. So are my former church leaders, my friend's ex-wife, and everyone I know.

As Paul says, "All have sinned and fall short of the glory of God."[19]

But the telos—the end goal, the aim—all throughout Scripture is clear. Love. "We love because he first loved us."[20]

So I press on expectantly, proudly writing as Micah E. (for Edward) Davis. The middle initial lives on as a reminder that when other people fail, God never does. I am the product of affair(s), abuse, lies, hiddenness, and abandonment. But I am also the child of a God who sees, loves, and knows me. I choose to live in my identity in Christ, rather than the sinful shame of my past. And you can too.

You can press on as a son or daughter of the One True King. All the hurt you've endured has formed you, sure. But you are so much more. Through Christ, you are a conqueror. And that redeemed state of your resurrected identity in Christ lies ahead.

Forgiveness is the key. Gratitude is the result. Eternity awaits.

Forgiveness sounds right. It even feels right—when we're the ones who benefit. But it often doesn't look right.

Jesus teaches on the subject of forgiveness many times throughout the Gospels.[21] Check out this interaction between Jesus and—yep, you guessed it—Peter. "Then Peter came to Jesus and asked, 'Lord, how many times shall I forgive my brother or sister who sins against me? Up to seven times?' Jesus answered, 'I tell you, not seven times, but seventy-seven times.'"[22]

Forgiveness sounds right. But those sentiments don't look right. Especially that last one.

To better understand this interaction between Peter and Jesus, it is useful to look at the historical context. As previously mentioned, in ancient Israel, Jewish rabbis taught that forgiveness need only be extended . . . three times. Seriously. After that one could simply break relationship and move on.

Seems not much has changed today, right?

So, to Peter, offering to forgive seven times (the "perfect" number) might have seemed generous. This was Peter puffing out his chest a bit and declaring, "Jesus, I know what they teach, but you suggest seven times, right?"[23]

And Jesus' response, once again, stuns everyone—no one more than Peter. "I tell you, not seven times, but seventy-seven times."[24] Other translations say seventy times seven times. Either way, Jesus is decimating the traditional teaching of his day.

The way of Jesus is adamantly clear. Forgiveness is for everyone. Even—especially—for those we consider our "enemies."

Here's Jesus in Matthew 5: "You have heard that it was said, 'Love your neighbor and hate your enemy.' But I tell you, love your enemies and pray for those who persecute you."[25]

To follow Jesus is to not just "talk the talk" of forgiveness but to actually walk it out. We can't call for *forgiveness* over and over again and not practice it. Eventually people will stop believing us. We must live it.

But how? This is incredibly difficult.

It is because of Jesus' death and resurrection that forgiveness, beyond three strikes, is possible. We serve a God who offers second, third, and fiftieth chances. He is a God who never gives up on you.

Let's return to the room where Jesus met the disciples after his resurrection. It's not lost on me that the disciples had deserted Jesus and hid for *three* days. When Jesus walked in, with every right to disown and disarm his followers for their lack of faith, their cowardice, their betrayal, he said, "Peace be with you."

"Peace be with you."

"Peace be with you."

One act of grace for every mistake. Jesus covers it all.

Forgiveness is always possible. It's not always fair, but it's always possible.

A few days after Jesus' death, burial, and resurrection, the Lord appears to Peter. This is the first recorded conversation we have between them since Peter's tragic failure in Mark 14, and here's how it goes:

> "Simon son of John, do you love me more than these?"
> "Yes, Lord," he said, "you know that I love you."
> Jesus said, "Feed my lambs."
> Again Jesus said, "Simon son of John, do you love me?"
> He answered, "Yes, Lord, you know that I love you."
> Jesus said, "Take care of my sheep."
> The third time he said to him, "Simon son of John, do you love me?"
> Peter was hurt because Jesus asked him the third time, "Do you love me?" He said, "Lord, you know all things; you know that I love you."
> Jesus said, "Feed my sheep."[26]

In case we're not tracking, Peter fell asleep three times. Peter denied Jesus three times. Jesus hung on a cross in darkness for three hours. Jesus lay in a tomb dead for three days. And then Jesus resurrected, conquering death, sin, and failure forever.

In the first recorded conversation post-Resurrection between Jesus and his disciples, he says a singular statement about peace three times. In the first recorded conversation post-Resurrection between Peter and Jesus, he asks Peter a simple question *three* times.

Notice that Peter was hurt after Jesus asked him the third time. Why? Because Peter was still operating by the standard Jewish law of his day. If someone asks you something three times, you've reached the limit. Three questions, he's out. Point blank. Period.

But Jesus was rewriting the script.

For every abandonment, every denial, every failure that Peter had committed . . . forgiveness was waiting for him.

The New International Version translation heads this passage with the title "Jesus Reinstates Peter," because that's exactly what is happening. Peter the denier, liar, and abandoner steps fully into the redeemed namesake Jesus gives him. The rock on which Jesus will build his church. "Then [Jesus] said to him, 'Follow me!'"[27]

Wouldn't you know, this is one of the last recorded lines to Peter in the Gospels. A new story is being written. One that picks up in Acts 2 when Peter addresses the crowd with the first sermon after Pentecost. Full of the Holy Spirit, Peter the rock goes on to build Christ's church.

As it turns out, failure isn't final. Forgiveness is.

Three strikes . . . you're forgiven.

Epilogue

A Legacy That Will Last

AS FATE WOULD HAVE IT, I am writing the concluding pages of this book on Good Friday. As I meditate and reflect on Jesus' journey to the Cross, I am struck by the lasting legacies that are preserved within the pages of Scripture.

There's Herod and his soldiers, excited to see Jesus up close and expectant for him to perform miracles, but sorely disappointed when he doesn't, leading them to mock and ridicule the Savior of the world.

There's Pilate, who, leaning on the strength of Rome, led weakly when pushed and prodded by the crowd. There are the chief priests, elected to be examples of holiness, instead becoming dark agents of strife.

There's the crowd, who days before were chanting, "Hosanna!" toward Jesus and are now chanting, "Crucify him! Crucify him!"[1]

And then there's Jesus . . . who, after enduring brutal mistreatment, begins his death sentence with these words: "Father, forgive them, for they do not know what they are doing."[2]

We mustn't miss the significance of this statement. If there is a crossroads where Jesus must choose whether to follow through on his promised sacrifice or give up and retreat to the safety of his divine throne, *this* is it. In a moment of mockery, after being whipped, beaten, and bruised, after carrying a treacherous cross to the hill of his execution, he cries out, "Father, forgive them."

These are the words that echo from the cross. Not "Father, rebuke them."

"Father, destroy them."

"Father, tell them that they're wrong."

"Father . . . *forgive* them."

In my most honest reflections, I'm unsure if I could bring myself to say the same. And yet this is why I am in need of a Savior. A Savior who can do what I can't do on my own. A Savior willing to forgive those who don't know what they are doing.

It is at the Cross that we witness heaven touching earth. The future glory of resurrection is communicated through Jesus' words of reconciliation. Only someone who can see the bigger, full picture can offer such words of forgiveness. As New Testament scholar N. T. Wright says, "Forgiveness brings the life of heaven to earth, God's future into the present."[3]

There is a future coming where those who were once enemies are now friends, where strangers are neighbors, and where rivals are joined arm in arm. There is a future where we extend God's grace freely to others and live eternally forgiven. If this is not the preferred future that we are working toward, then we must ask if the Savior who casts forgiveness down from the cross is the Savior we truly follow.

Forgiveness is required, but not everyone is obedient to Jesus' teaching. Jesus, in his kindness, has given us free will to choose. But to leave a legacy is inevitable. We will be remembered by *someone* for *something*. We must decide if forgiveness will be included in our eulogy.

If it isn't, there is a price to pay. As the spiritual writer Henri Nouwen once said, "A forgiven person forgives."[4] Could it be that you haven't fully embraced being forgiven? Could the bondage that has ensnared you throughout life be rooted in bitterness and resentment? Could your inability to forgive be holding you back from the freedom you long for? What if you could choose another way?

The question, of course, is how do we get started?

At this point, we have covered some ground. We've looked at how we start at different points in our forgiveness journey—but we don't have to stay there. How we can acknowledge the hurt in our past and then begin the ongoing process of forgiving others. How we can embrace the truth that forgiveness redeems our past and is ultimately for our good.

We've walked through forgiving as both a practice and a process. We've looked at how forgiveness can be marked by an instantaneous action or declaration, but the process of working through the emotions and pursuing reconciliation takes time. Sitting in the messiness of that process is painful but worth it. Over time, we become—as Nouwen terms it—wounded healers who are able to transform pain rather than transfer it.[5] Often, the most difficult person to forgive in all of this is ourselves. But God already sees you as forgiven if you've put your faith and hope in Jesus. He's simply asking you to believe him. This is easier said than done, so we cling to the prayer of a father from Mark 9: "I do believe; help me overcome my unbelief!"[6]

All of this is the foundation for becoming practitioners of forgiveness. Forgiveness can't remain an ideal or a theory; it must be worked out in the real situations of day-to-day life.

Because of sin, we all start from a place of brokenness. Our stories are to be handled with care. We must examine the ways that we have fallen short and humbly ask for forgiveness when we've hurt someone else. But we don't have to remain in a place of guilt or shame. Once we've admitted our sin, we are released from our debt and freed to embrace all that God has for us. This isn't always easy. There have certainly been pieces of our past—scripts that were written—that have marked us. There have been assumptions that these scripts have forced us to carry. We might still wrestle with receiving or extending forgiveness. And it's all under the big question: "Does God even care?"

But forgiveness—as we said—is for everyone. This is unfair . . . *and it is good news!* My friend, even when you fail over and over again, like the disciples and Peter did, Jesus tells us, "Peace be with you." He returns with a message of grace and establishes our purpose. Failure isn't final. It's not the end of your story. Forgiveness doesn't just redeem our past; it restores our present. God cares deeply for you. He has already forgiven you and called you into a new way of life—a way of forgiveness. We live in a culture that lusts on the failure of others. But prophetically, we can lead others into a different way. A way marked by unearned grace and mercy, with justice in tow. A way where we can forgive in response to all that we've been forgiven for.

Day after day, over time, forgiving as we've been forgiven helps to secure our future. A future where ultimate reconciliation takes place. Where relationships are restored, lives are healed, and life is found. This future is for everyone, yes, everyone who repents and believes in the Good News of Jesus Christ. And its transformative power is available to us now as we work toward a forgiving future in a failing present.

Over the course of my life, I have been haunted by failure. I was the kid who never got a hit. I swung and missed over and over and over again. And that umpire's gravel yell still gets stuck in my head sometimes.

"Three strikes, you're *OUT!*"

Maybe that voice comes for you, too, at times.

But when we get to the end of our lives, in the bottom of the ninth inning, the last fastball will be thrown, and the Umpire of life will shockingly, sweetly, call out, "Three strikes, you'reeeeee . . . *forgiven.*"

Thanks

THIS BOOK WAS BORN out of a teaching reflecting on pain. A few hours later, Sarah A. at Tyndale told me *that* teaching was the basis for my next book. I never thought I'd ever be asked to write on a topic as weighty as forgiveness, but I'm grateful to Sarah for believing that I had this in me all those years ago.

A special thank-you to

- Paul Akhimien
- Elijah Davis
- Rylei Davis
- Christian Dawson
- Brieyonna Gamble
- Braden Ochs
- Ryan Olson
- Matt Siewert

who read individual chapters of the earliest version of this manuscript and offered kind, compassionate critique that allowed this work to find its final form.

And a very special thank-you to Victoria Ochs, who pored over the first version of this manuscript in full. I so admire your ability to notice places for nuance and your care for the least, the last, and the lost. You make my sermons better weekly, and you've made this book better too.

Ian Simkins—for your belief in and support of me and this work in particular. Words can't express how much I look up to you. Thanks for modeling what it looks like to pastor, father, husband, and follow Jesus *well*.

Claire Lloyd—for catching the vision for this and fighting for what's necessary.

Dan Balow—I still can't believe you took a chance on a twenty-five-year-old kid. To see where we've come . . .

Kara Leonino, Stephanie Abrassart, and the entire Tyndale Team—you guys make this process so incredibly fun.

Libby Dykstra and Laura Cruise—Jedi master designers. This is a beautiful piece.

Sibyl and Dick Towner and The Springs staff—spiritual direction, walks in the labyrinth, prayer in the chapel . . . I cherish all of it. See you next month.

The Sanctuary—church family, it's hard to put into words how much has changed in just a few years. What was once a dream is now a reality. And it is so much sweeter than I ever could have dared imagine. Until Indianapolis looks like heaven . . .

Jake Hirsch—y'know, for basically everything.

The Sanctuary's Staff and Board—for championing my unique calling as a pastor/writer, writer/pastor and empowering me to live into this.

The Brotherhood—Tom, Slav, Jordan, Nick, Caleb, Aaron, Jenson. The company of pastors inspiring me in so many ways. Onward.

CC—in it through thick and thin. Happy birthday, Hallie and Walt. Uncle M loves you.

Walsh's—for the sacred space and slow days, oh and an author picture that my wife *really* likes.

Lij, Zay, J&J—I'm for you, always.

Mom and Dad—for staying together, doing the hard work, and modeling forgiveness and reconciliation over and over . . . and over again.

Ry—for choosing me even when I fall short. Your love teaches me so much about Jesus'. I love you. Forever and ever.

Writing a book is a laborious, time-consuming, pedantic process. It goes in starts and stops, over years, distilling ideas into actual words on pages. This would not be possible without the help of so many of the people mentioned above and others that I may have missed.

Overall, I am just so, so grateful.

Appendix A

A Note of Consideration Regarding Abuse

I WANT TO ENSURE THAT I OFFER a clear, direct clarification regarding forgiveness and abuse. My heart goes out to anyone reading this whose story contains abuse of any kind.

It is important to state here that forgiveness does not mean forgetfulness. As you work toward forgiving your abuser, there should be zero expectation to excuse, explain, or justify their actions. When abuse and power dynamics are present in a particular relationship, forgiveness is not as cut-and-dried as "because the Bible tells me so." There is a mountain of complex emotions that must be waded through in this process. Biblical forgiveness is not the absence of justice, accountability, or righteous anger. In fact, these aspects of the forgiveness journey are often key components to true healing taking place.

Forgiving your abuser doesn't mean continuing to be in close or intimate relationship with them. In fact, it may be healthiest and safest if there is physical distance between you and them for a set period of time (perhaps for the rest of your life). While God's heart is always for reconciliation, sometimes this simply is not possible in our broken, sinful, fallen world. Reconciliation requires repentance. If the abuser is unwilling to repent, acknowledge the severity of their decisions, and change their behavior, reconciliation is a nonstarter. Understand that this is not your fault. It's theirs. Please grieve this unfortunate reality, but do not carry shame or blame for it. You can seek healing and wholeness for yourself in spite of their inability to do the same.

If your abuser does express genuine repentance and remorse, this also does not mean that you must fully restore your relationship immediately or perhaps ever to the same degree it was originally. Choices have consequences that need to be faced. The hope in forgiveness is not that you would desire close relationship with them. The hope in forgiveness is that you would see resentment, hatred, and anger subside in your heart and that your life would be marked by forgiveness, love, and freedom instead of bitterness.

So, if abuse is a part of your story, I am incredibly sorry. It grieves me and grieves the heart of God. But your abuse does not have to be the definitive mark of your life. We serve a God who sees you, loves you, and longs to restore the shattered pieces of your heart and make them whole. Forgiveness is a difficult journey, but it is worthwhile—and brings healing.

Appendix B

Verses on Forgiveness

I HAVE FOUND THAT on particular days being able to locate what God's Word says about forgiveness is extremely helpful and comforting. And so, I've taken time to compile what the Bible has to say regarding forgiveness in the order that the verses occur canonically. I hope and pray they bring peace and hope to your soul in times of need.

Genesis 50:17	Psalm 19:12
Exodus 10:17	Psalm 25:11
Exodus 23:21	Psalm 32:5
Exodus 32:32	Psalm 79:9
Exodus 34:9	Psalm 86:5
Numbers 14:19	Psalm 103:10-14
1 Samuel 15:25	Psalm 130:4
1 Kings 8:30	Proverbs 28:13
1 Kings 8:50	Isaiah 1:18
2 Chronicles 6:21	Isaiah 53:5
2 Chronicles 7:14	Isaiah 55:7

Jeremiah 5:7	Acts 2:38
Jeremiah 31:34	Acts 3:19
Jeremiah 33:8	Acts 5:31
Jeremiah 50:20	Acts 10:43
Daniel 9:19	Romans 8:1
Hosea 14:2	Romans 12:18
Micah 7:18-19	Romans 12:14, 15-17, 19
Matthew 5:23-24	2 Corinthians 2:5-11
Matthew 6:9-15	2 Corinthians 5:18, 20
Matthew 18:15-18	Ephesians 1:7
Matthew 18:21-22	Ephesians 4:31-32
Matthew 18:35	Colossians 1:13-14
Matthew 26:28	Colossians 3:13
Mark 2:10	2 Timothy 3:1-5
Mark 11:25	Hebrews 8:12
Luke 5:24	Hebrews 10:17
Luke 6:37	Hebrews 12:14-15
Luke 11:4	1 Peter 2:21
Luke 17:3-4	1 Peter 2:23
Luke 19:8	1 John 1:9
Luke 23:34	1 John 2:1
John 17:20-23	1 John 2:3, 6, 9-10
John 20:23	

Appendix C

Other Helpful Resources

FORGIVENESS IS A SENSITIVE SUBJECT. I have labored to craft a piece of work that is helpful and hopeful to any and all who read it. But I am not able to cover everything. I have found these resources helpful in my journey of forgiveness. I share them with those of you who would like to continue on this journey with voices other than my own. I pray their words supplement my words—in partnership with God's Word—to bring healing and wholeness to you.

I Forgive You by Wendy Alsup

Forgiveness After Trauma by Susannah Griffith

Forgive by Timothy Keller

Forgiveness by Sidney B. Simon and Suzanne Simon

Experiencing Forgiveness by Charles F. Stanley

Forgiving What You Can't Forget by Lysa Terkeurst

No Future Without Forgiveness by Desmond Tutu

The Book of Forgiving by Desmond Tutu and Mpho Tutu

Forgiving and Reconciling by Everett L. Worthington Jr.

The Power of Forgiving by Everett L. Worthington Jr.

Notes

PROLOGUE: I'VE BEEN THROUGH IT

1. For those unfamiliar with my family's story, you can read about it in my parents' memoir, *Beyond Ordinary*. I don't unpack much of it in this book, as it's their story to tell, not mine.
2. Micah E. Davis, *Trailblazers: A Journey to Discover God's Purpose for Your Life* (Tyndale House, 2023).
3. Genesis 50:20.
4. Genesis 16:13.
5. Matthew 6:14-15.
6. Matthew 11:28-30, MSG.

CHAPTER 1: THE STARTING POINT

1. i.e., those who have repented, believed, and received Jesus as Lord.
2. For further context, please see Appendix A: A Note of Consideration Regarding Abuse.
3. I am indebted to Dr. Brandon Shields, who has taken me under his wing and taught me so much about being and becoming a more trauma-informed pastor. Love my Soma family.
4. Romans 3:23; 6:23.
5. Galatians 5:22.
6. This isn't a necessary detail; I just thought you should know. I've surrendered to the inevitable truth, okay?

7. Fun fact: Joel played without a tooth for a few months until Christmas break. He's literally the only person who could pull that off and still look good. Ugh.

8. The Substance Abuse and Mental Health Services Administration (SAMHSA) defines trauma as "an event or circumstance resulting in physical harm, emotional harm, and/or life-threatening harm" that "has adverse effects on the individual's mental health, physical health, emotional health, social well-being, and/or spiritual well-being." "Trauma and Violence," SAMHSA, accessed November 12, 2024, https://www.samhsa.gov/trauma-violence.

9. That's a joke. I was—and am—the worst defender on the planet. I make no excuses. I hate defense.

10. Matthew 11:30.

11. Blue Letter Bible, s.v. "chrēstos (*adj.*)," accessed November 4, 2024, https://www.blueletterbible.org/lexicon/g5543/kjv/tr/0-1/.

12. John 16:33.

13. Blue Letter Bible, s.v. "thlipsis (*n.*)," accessed November 4, 2024, https://www.blueletterbible.org/lexicon/g2347/kjv/tr/0-1/.

14. A Jay-Z reference for all you cultured people. An *Annie* reference for those that are not. Kidding!

15. Isaiah 53:4-5.

16. Mark 15:34.

17. Thanks for this beautiful truth, Brandon Shields.

18. If you need help to get started, our church has created a resource for people locally here in Indianapolis to find counseling, but it also contains options that are virtual and can be accessed by anyone, anywhere. You can find it here: www.sanctuaryindy.com/resources.

19. John 20:25.

20. John 20:25.

21. John 11:7-8.

22. John 11:16.

23. John 20:26-27.

24. John 20:28.

25. Matthew 8:15.

26. John 20:26.

27. Psalm 34:8.

CHAPTER 2: FAMILY TREES

1. "Stay in the Magic . . . and Play!," Walt Disney World, accessed November 5, 2024, https://disneyworld.disney.go.com/vacation-planning/.
2. As noted in the phenomenal documentary *More Than a Game* that follows LeBron and his teammates throughout this tournament and beyond.
3. "Supposed to be" because my dad spent most of the time mad at me for refusing to ride roller coasters. "Why are we here if you're not going to ride a roller coaster?" I'm terrified of heights and fast things. Roller coasters are a no-go for me. However, he ended up bribing me with a pair of Beats headphones if I complied. I rode my first and only roller coaster (on purpose) that day.
4. Genesis 12:10-20; 20.
5. Genesis 27.
6. Genesis 25:26.
7. Genesis 37.
8. 2 Samuel 3:2-5; 1 Chronicles 3:1-3; 2 Samuel 5:13.
9. 1 Kings 11:3.
10. 2 Chronicles 11:21.
11. You can read Joseph's story in Genesis 37–45. I also go more in depth into Joseph's story in chapter 1 of *Trailblazers*.
12. Genesis 45:2.
13. Genesis 50:20-21.
14. Genesis 25–33 will give you the account in full if you're interested.
15. Genesis 32:6.
16. Genesis 32:20.
17. Genesis 33:4.
18. Genesis 20:1-2.
19. Genesis 26:7-9.
20. Genesis 27.
21. Genesis 33:2-3.
22. For a more in-depth study of the genogram, check out Peter Scazzero's *Emotionally Healthy Spirituality*, which has been a highly formative book in my own spiritual journey.

23. Colossians 3:12.

24. 1 John 4:19.

25. Isaiah 53:5.

26. C. S. Lewis, "On Forgiveness," in *The Weight of Glory and Other Addresses* (HarperOne, 1980), 182.

27. Revelation 3:20.

CHAPTER 3: THE CYCLE OF FORGIVENESS

1. Justin and Trisha Davis, "No Ordinary Forgiveness," *Today's Christian Woman*, March 2013, https://www.todayschristianwoman.com/articles/2013/march/no-ordinary-forgiveness.html.

2. Exodus 34:6-7.

3. Micah 6:8.

4. Genesis 3:9.

5. Matthew 6:12, 14-15.

6. Matthew 7:1-2.

7. Hannah Montana, "Nobody's Perfect," YouTube, 3:24, December 10, 2010, https://www.youtube.com/watch?v=t93u0qg5q_M.

8. Romans 3:23.

9. Matthew 5:7, 9.

10. Romans 3:23.

11. Peter Scazzero with Warren Bird, *The Emotionally Healthy Church: A Strategy for Discipleship That Actually Changes Lives* (Zondervan, 2003), 157.

12. Jerry L. Sittser, "Jerry Sittser on the Early Church 'Third Way, Re-introducing a Christian Imagination, and Navigating Grief through a Redemptive Lens," *Canadian Church Leaders Podcast*, February 26, 2024, https://www.ccln.ca/podcast/2024/jerrysittser.

13. Psalm 34:18.

14. A caveat—working toward rebuilding does not necessarily mean immediate trust or even relational proximity if safety is a concern. For situations involving abuse, see appendix A.

15. 2 Corinthians 2:5-11.

CHAPTER 4: TRANSFORMED ASSUMPTIONS

1. Aumyo Hassan and Sarah J. Barber, "The Effects of Repetition Frequency on the Illusory Truth Effect," *Cognitive Research: Principles and Implications* 6, no. 38 (May 13, 2021), https://www.ncbi.nlm.nih.gov/pmc/articles/PMC8116821/.
2. Genesis 7:2-3.
3. Mark 4:36, emphasis mine.
4. You're not getting a book without a Star Wars reference. Sorry not sorry.
5. Matthew 20:1-2.
6. Matthew 20:4-5.
7. Matthew 20:9-16.
8. Bible Hub, s.v. "enomisan," accessed November 5, 2024, https://biblehub.com/greek/enomisan_3543.htm.
9. John Ortberg, *Soul Keeping: Caring for the Most Important Part of You* (Zondervan, 2014), 147.
10. Matthew 6:14-15.
11. Mark 8:35.
12. Mark 10:43-44.
13. Matthew 20:16.
14. Matthew 7:5.
15. Matthew 20:15.
16. Bible Hub, s.v. "ponēros," accessed November 5, 2024, https://biblehub.com/greek/pone_ros_4190.htm.
17. Psalm 139:23-24.
18. Matthew 20:16.

CHAPTER 5: FAILURE OBSESSED

1. Or maybe after you finish this chapter.
2. Conor Friedersdorf, "The Real Reason Cancel Culture Is So Contentious," *Atlantic*, April 28, 2022, https://www.theatlantic.com/ideas/archive/2022/04/cancel-culture-debate-needs-greater-specificity/629654/.
3. Peg Moline, "We're Far More Afraid of Failure Than Ghosts: Here's How to Stare It Down," *Los Angeles Times*, October 31, 2015, https://www.latimes.com/health/la-he-scared-20151031-story.html.

4. John 8:3.

5. John 8:3-4.

6. Bible Hub, s.v. "histémi," accessed November 6, 2024, https://biblehub.com/greek/2476.htm.

7. John 8:5.

8. John 8:6.

9. Philippians 2:6-8.

10. Tony Evans, *The Tony Evans Bible Commentary* (Holman Bible, 2019), 1,035.

11. *The Chronicles of Narnia: The Lion, the Witch, and the Wardrobe*, directed by Andrew Adamson (Walden Media, 2005), DVD.

12. John 8:11.

13. Romans 8:1.

14. John 8:7-8.

15. John 8:10-11.

16. John 8:11.

17. I'm grateful to my friends and the elders at Bridgetown Church, who have graciously allowed us at The Sanctuary to adopt this part of their statement of belief as our own. It is a beautiful, poetic summary on how Jesus so brilliantly balanced the tension of day-to-day life.

18. "John 8," Bible Hub, accessed November 6, 2024, https://biblehub.com/interlinear/john/8.htm.

19. Corrie ten Boom, "Guideposts Classics: Corrie ten Boom on Forgiveness," *Guideposts*, November 1972, https://guideposts.org/positive-living/guideposts-classics-corrie-ten-boom-forgiveness/.

20. Ten Boom, "On Forgiveness."

21. Ten Boom, "On Forgiveness."

22. Ten Boom, "On Forgiveness."

23. John 8:7.

24. Matthew 7:1-2.

25. Matthew 7:3-5.

26. John 8:58-59.

27. For instance, Matthew 16:23; Matthew 18:15; Matthew 23:29-31;

Matthew 25:31-46; Ephesians 5:11; 1 Timothy 5:20; 2 Timothy 4:2; Titus 1:13; Revelation 3:14-19.

CHAPTER 6: COME OUT OF HIDING

1. 1 Kings 3:6.
2. 1 Samuel 16:12.
3. 2 Samuel 11:1-5.
4. 2 Samuel 11:6-13.
5. 2 Samuel 11:14-27.
6. You can read the story in full in 2 Samuel 12.
7. Romans 3:23-24.
8. Psalm 51:1-2. If you'd like, it's worth reading all of Psalm 51.
9. Blue Letter Bible, "metanoeō (v.)," accessed November 7, 2024, https://www.blueletterbible.org/lexicon/g3340/kjv/tr/0-1/.
10. A mantra from a mentor of mine, Steve Carter. Thanks for living this out for me, Steve.
11. As an Enneagram 3 with a core vice of "deceiving," I am exceptional at this. Please understand, this is nothing to brag about. Rather, this is a self-awareness that I have gained over the last decade. To deny or dismiss this reality is to only play further into my false self that I am constantly seeking to break free from.
12. Hebrews 10:19-22.
13. Psalm 103:10-11, ESV.

CHAPTER 7: PUT IT TO USE

1. Matthew Thomas, Spotify playlist, accessed November 7, 2024, https://open.spotify.com/artist/7nXc5GnVamvOQljnboMFki?si=gfO6WR-IToicwjtmoZFO_A.
2. Some people also define forgiveness as "to stop being angry about a wrong thing someone has done to you and to forget about it." However, I fundamentally disagree with this definition, as I argue extensively throughout this work.
3. Matthew 6:12.
4. Trisha Winter, "Forgive as Jesus Forgives," Centralia Community Church, March 28, 2021, https://cccog.com/beyond-sunday/2021/3/29/forgive-as-jesus-forgives.

5. Matthew 18:23-24.
6. "Matthew 18—Qualities and Attitudes of Kingdom Citizens," Enduring Word, accessed November 7, 2024, https://enduringword.com/bible-commentary/matthew-18/.
7. Matthew 18:25-26.
8. Matthew 18:27.
9. "Matthew 18," Enduring Word.
10. Matthew 18:28-30.
11. Matthew 18:31-34.
12. Matthew 18:35.
13. Matthew 5:7.
14. Matthew 15:22.
15. Luke 17:13.
16. Matthew 20:30.
17. Psalm 51:17.
18. Luke 17:3, ESV.
19. Matthew 5:23-24, ESV.
20. Acts 2:38; Acts 3:19; James 5:16; 1 John 1:9.
21. Isabel Goddard, "What Does Friendship Look Like in America?" Pew Research Center, October 12, 2023, https://www.pewresearch.org/short-reads/2023/10/12/what-does-friendship-look-like-in-america.
22. Martin Luther King Jr., "Loving Your Enemies" in *Strength to Love* (Fortress Press, 1981), 51.
23. Love you, Steve Carter.
24. James 5:16.
25. This was originally "listen, then speak," but then my friend Jay Y. Kim sent me his new book entitled *Listen, Listen, Speak*, and I am hooked. All love, J Kim!
26. Matthew 7:3-5.
27. See "Morning Prayer from *The Book of Common Prayer*," *Common Worship*, Church House, The Archbishops' Council of the Church of England, 2000–2004, accessed November 7, 2024, http://justus.anglican.org/~ss/commonworship/word/morningbcp.html.
28. Romans 8:1.

CHAPTER 8: EMBRACING WHAT WE AVOID

1. Genesis 1:27-28.
2. Romans 7:15.
3. Michael Jordan, "Failure," Nike commercial, 1997, YouTube, 0:30, https://www.youtube.com/watch?v=45mMioJ5szc.
4. Hebrews 12:2, emphasis mine.
5. Caty Medrano, "Top 10 Strong Human Fears," September 30, 2011, https://listverse.com/2011/09/30/top-10-strong-human-fears/.
6. Other than fear of the Lord. If you're a follower of Jesus, perhaps you've come across the cliché that there's 365 "fear not" verses throughout the Bible. Sorry to break it to you, but that's a myth. In fact, some of those "fear not" verses bring not comfort but angst.
7. 2 Timothy 1:7, NLT.
8. Joshua 1:9.
9. John 16:33, THE VOICE.
10. Genesis 15:1.
11. Psalm 46:1.
12. Genesis 3:1.
13. John 14:6.
14. Luke 19:10.
15. Matthew 28:16-17, emphasis mine.
16. Matthew 28:18-20.
17. Dallas Willard, *The Great Omission: Reclaiming Jesus's Essential Teachings on Discipleship* (HarperCollins, 2006), 61.
18. John 3:16.
19. Romans 8:11.
20. Matthew 16:24.

CHAPTER 9: THE HARDEST PERSON TO FORGIVE

1. Genesis 37:3.
2. "Joseph," The Biblical Timeline, accessed November 7, 2024, https://www.thebiblicaltimeline.org/joseph/.
3. Genesis 45:4-7.

4. Genesis 50:14-15.

5. Genesis 50:16-17.

6. John 3:16.

7. Genesis 50:17.

8. 1 John 4:9-10; 1 Peter 5:7; Psalm 121:8; Luke 15:4.

9. Genesis 50:18.

10. Colossians 3:13.

11. Ephesians 1:7.

12. Acts 10:43.

13. Luke 6:36.

14. Genesis 50:19-21.

15. Matthew 26:28.

16. Genesis 3:9.

17. 1 John 1:9.

18. Justin Taylor, "Tozer vs. Lewis: What's the Most Important Thing about Us?," The Gospel Coalition, June 4, 2016, https://www.thegospelcoalition.org/blogs/justin-taylor/tozer-vs-lewis-whats-the-most-important-thing-about-us/.

19. Genesis 50:21.

20. Everett Worthington, "Six Steps to Forgiving Yourself," accessed October 15, 2024, https://www.evworthington-forgiveness.com/six-steps-to-forgiving-yourself.

CHAPTER 10: THE BIG QUESTION

1. Luke 1:18.

2. Luke 1:34.

3. John 6:9.

4. Matthew 28:16-17, emphasis mine.

5. Isaiah 55:8.

6. Let me add that from a theological perspective, God does not *need* our forgiveness. His ways are perfect. He is perfect. But from a relational perspective, it is difficult for us to love someone we do not trust. Forgiveness—I've found—is the pathway to learning to trust God, especially when his ways do not align with my ways.

7. Matthew 26:39.

8. Matthew 27:46.

9. John 3:16.

10. Matthew 26:39.

11. Rich Plass, "Pastors Forum," Practicing the Way, May 31, 2023, https://www.practicingtheway.org/.

12. Psalm 89:26.

13. Psalm 22:1-2.

14. Psalm 13:1-3; 44:23-24; 79:5, 10.

15. Psalm 22:3-5.

16. John Ortberg, *Soul Keeping: Caring for the Most Important Part of You* (Zondervan, 2014), 147.

17. This according to the fashion transparency organization Good On You.

18. Isaiah 53:3.

19. 1 Peter 3:14; 1 Peter 4:1; 2 Timothy 3:12; James 1:2-3; James 1:12.

20. Ronald Rolheiser, interview by John Mark Comer, posted October 4, 2023, Practicing the Way, Vimeo, https://vimeo.com/871265124/0c9d2d7867.

21. This quote is widely attributed to Gandhi.

22. I recognize that for some reading this, it may not be healthy or even safe to return to the church you've left. Please understand when I say return, I mean to a church community. I can't pretend to know or cover all of the complexity and nuance in your specific situation, but the local church is a vital part of your spiritual formation. It is my pastoral repainting to gently push you back into the fray of God's family. So please, consider these words!

23. *Interstellar*, directed by Christopher Nolan (Paramount Pictures, 2014). Dylan Thomas, "Do Not Go Gentle into That Good Night," *The Collected Poems of Dylan Thomas* (New Directions, 1957).

CHAPTER 11: A FORGIVING FUTURE IN A FAILING PRESENT

1. Micah 6:1-2.

2. Micah 6:3-5.

3. Genesis 3:1.

4. Brown-Driver-Briggs Hebrew Lexicon, s.v. "shâkach (v.)," accessed November 8, 2024, https://www.bibletools.org/index.cfm/fuseaction/Lexicon.show/ID/H7911/shakach.htm.

5. Blue Letter Bible, s.v. "shâkach (v.)," accessed November 8, 2024, https://www.blueletterbible.org/lexicon/h7911/rsv/wlc/0-1/.

6. Deuteronomy 4:9, emphasis mine.

7. Deuteronomy 4:23-24, emphasis mine.

8. Isaiah 17:10, emphasis mine.

9. Ezekiel 23:35, emphasis mine.

10. Micah 6:6-7.

11. Micah 6:8.

12. Matthew 5:17.

13. Matthew 22:37-40.

14. Matthew 7:15-20.

15. John 13:35.

16. Romans 13:8.

17. Romans 10:9.

18. 2 Peter 3:11-13.

19. Matthew 16:24.

20. John 16:33.

21. Matthew 5:6.

22. Ronald Rolheiser, interview by John Mark Comer, posted October 4, 2023, Practicing the Way, Vimeo, https://vimeo.com/871265124/0c9d2d7867.

23. Derwin L. Gray, *God, Do You Hear Me?: Discover the Prayer God Always Answers* (B&H, 2021), 72.

24. James 2:12-13.

25. Galatians 6:7; Habakkuk 1:13.

26. Philippians 2:7-8.

27. André Guichaoua, "Counting the Rwandan Victims of War and Genocide: Concluding Reflections," *Journal of Genocide Research* 22, no. 1 (2020): 125–141, https://doi.org/10.1080/14623528.2019.1703329.

28. Susan Dominus, "Portraits of Reconciliation," *New York Times Magazine*, April 6, 2014, https://www.nytimes.com/interactive/2014/04/06/magazine/06-pieter-hugo-rwanda-portraits.html.

29. Judy Woodruff, Frank Carlson, and Sarah Clune Hartman, "Historian Compares America's Current Divisions to the Past and How We Can Overcome Them," PBS News, October 25, 2023, https://www.pbs.org/newshour/show/historian-compares-americas-current-divisions-to-the-past-and-how-we-can-overcome-them. Simon Jackman, "America More Divided Than at Any Time since Civil War," United States Studies Centre, March 15, 2022, https://www.ussc.edu.au/america-more-divided-than-at-any-time-since-civil-war.

30. Charles Duhigg, "The Real Roots of American Rage," *Atlantic*, January/February 2019, https://www.theatlantic.com/magazine/archive/2019/01/charles-duhigg-american-anger/576424/.

31. Jon Tyson, "What to Do with Your Wounds," Jon Tyson Archive, accessed November 12, 2024, https://jontysonarchive.com/jon-tyson-archive/blog-post-title-one-wpmwe-x6arh-9e4fb-39tjr-h6kmn-g4x9c-t9tgg-f6fh9-psybz-myltd-sks34-fbzc6-fxy9l-pjbpy-342aa-ll7hz-5ypj4-fbf8c-xp9cb-ajhjs-4hw88-sftrt-3zpxw.

32. Thanks, Mom. :) Justin and Trisha Davis, "No Ordinary Forgiveness," *Today's Christian Woman*, March 2013, https://www.todayschristianwoman.com/articles/2013/march/no-ordinary-forgiveness.html.

33. 2 Corinthians 5:20.

CHAPTER 12: FORGIVENESS IS FOR EVERYONE (YES, EVERYONE)

1. Luke 23:43.
2. Luke 23:35-36, 39.
3. Luke 23:40-41.
4. Luke 23:42.
5. Luke 23:43.
6. John 20:19.
7. John 20:22-23.
8. Hebrew, meaning "peace."
9. John 20:23.
10. Matthew 6:14-15, emphasis mine.
11. Luke 6:37.

12. Mark 11:25.

13. Luke 17:3-4, emphasis mine.

14. Matthew 6:15.

15. Luke 23:43.

16. Henri J. M. Nouwen, *The Road to Daybreak: A Spiritual Journey* (Image Books, 1990), 68.

17. Headings adapted from Timothy Keller, *Forgive: Why Should I and How Can I?* (Penguin Books, 2023). Insights are my own.

18. A thought-provoking opinion article written by Maha Hilal brings our more than twenty-year war in the Middle East into serious ethical question, especially for the nonviolent follower of Jesus. Read here: Maha Hilal, "9/11 Anniversary: When 'Never Forget' Is Used to Justify the 'Forever War,'" Middle East Eye, September 12, 2022, https://www.middleeasteye.net/opinion/september-11-never-forget-justify-forever-war.

19. Psalm 103:11-12, emphasis mine.

20. Psalm 33:5.

21. Galatians 6:1.

22. Keller, *Forgive*, 170.

23. I recognize this is a bit blunt, but I am not being sarcastic. Unfortunately, there is extensive evidence in and throughout church history (especially recently) where this tactic has been used, and it is evil.

24. "Church of the Highlands Opens $4.5 Million 'Pastoral Recovery' Center. What Is It?," National Newspaper Publishers Association, accessed November 8, 2024, https://nnpa.org/church-of-the-highlands-opens-4-5-million-pastoral-recovery-center-what-is-it/.

25. Colossians 3:13.

26. Charles F. Stanley, *Experiencing Forgiveness: Enjoy the Peace of Giving and Receiving Grace* (Thomas Nelson, 2019), 11, the words "the act" emphasis mine.

27. Lysa Terkeurst, *Forgiving What You Can't Forget: Discover How to Move On, Make Peace with Painful Memories, and Create a Life That's Beautiful Again* (Nelson Books, 2020), emphasis mine.

28. Matthew 6:14-15.

29. Luke 23:33-34.

30. My paraphrase of Luke 23:38-42.

31. Luke 23:43.

32. John 20:26, emphasis mine.

33. Corrie ten Boom, "Guideposts Classics: Corrie ten Boom on Forgiveness," *Guideposts*, November 1972, https://guideposts.org/positive-living/guideposts-classics-corrie-ten-boom-forgiveness/.

34. John 3:16.

CHAPTER 13: THREE STRIKES, YOU'RE FORGIVEN

1. Mark 14:27-28.
2. Mark 14:29-31, emphasis mine.
3. Mark 14:32.
4. Mark 14:37-38.
5. Mark 14:40.
6. Mark 14:41.
7. Mark 14:68.
8. Mark 14:69, MSG.
9. Mark 14:70.
10. Mark 14:71.
11. Mark 14:72.
12. Matthew 27:45.
13. Matthew 5:23-24.
14. Luke 23:34.
15. Ephesians 4:31-32.
16. Matthew 5:44.
17. Mark 11:25.
18. Genesis 50:20.
19. Romans 3:23.
20. 1 John 4:19.
21. Matthew 6:14-15; Luke 6:37; Mark 11:25; Luke 17:3-4.
22. Matthew 18:21-22.
23. Luke 17:3-4.
24. Matthew 18:22.
25. Matthew 5:43-44.

26. John 21:15-17.

27. John 21:19.

EPILOGUE: A LEGACY THAT WILL LAST

1. Luke 23:21.

2. Luke 23:34.

3. N. T. Wright, *Luke for Everyone* (Westminster John Knox Press, 2004), 284.

4. Henri Nouwen, "A Forgiven Person Forgives," Henri Nouwen Society, October 25, 2024, https://henrinouwen.org/meditations/a-forgiven-person-forgives/.

5. Henri J. M. Nouwen, *The Wounded Healer: Ministry in Contemporary Society* (Image Doubleday, 2010).

6. Mark 9:24.

About

HEY THERE!

A bit about me...

I live and write inside "the loop" of Indianapolis, Indiana, with my wife, Rylei, and our Australian kelpie, Leo.

I'm the pastor of teaching and vision at The Sanctuary.

I'm the author of *Trailblazers: A Journey to Discover God's Purpose for Your Life*.

I believe that the written and spoken word are mediums to elicit heart change and life transformation. I've committed my life to using words for *good*.

Thanks for joining me on this journey. I hope and pray this work has blessed you in some way.

WHAT NEXT?

Good books deserve to be shared.

If you've found this work helpful, it would mean the world to me if you'd consider

- posting a review at your favorite online bookseller;
- posting a picture on social media about why you enjoyed the book;
- sending a note to a friend who you think would benefit from this work. Or, even better, gifting them a copy yourself.

After a good read, I'm always looking for more. If it's helpful to you, below is a QR code to access more of my teachings and writings on faith, formation, and the life of Jesus.

You can also learn more at sanctuaryindy.com or by visiting micahedavis.com.

May the peace of Christ be upon you,

ALSO AVAILABLE FROM
MICAH E. DAVIS

TRAILBLAZERS

"Full of wisdom....
I wholeheartedly
recommend this book."
CARLOS WHITTAKER
author of *How to Human*

MICAH E. DAVIS

A journey
to discover
God's purpose
for your life

Visit TyndaleChristianResources.com for
the accompanying video teaching series.

Available wherever books are sold

CP2042

TYNDALE CHRISTIAN RESOURCES

Bible-Based Christian Resources That Equip and Inspire!

Helpful and Knowledgeable Bible Teachers You Can Trust

Your first stop for all streaming video curriculum available from Tyndale House Publishers to resource the church and the discipleship of believers.

TyndaleChristianResources.com

ALSO AVAILABLE FROM
MICAH E. DAVIS

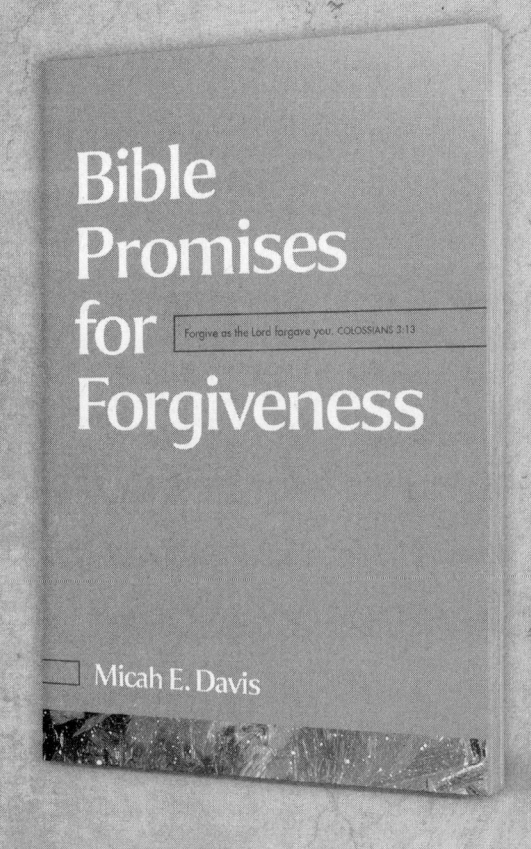

Bible Promises for Forgiveness

Forgive as the Lord forgave you. COLOSSIANS 3:13

Micah E. Davis

AVAILABLE EVERYWHERE BOOKS ARE SOLD